SPEECHES and SCENES from OSCAR'S BEST FILMS

SPEECHES and SCENES
from
OSCAR'S BEST FILMS

Edited by Dick Dotterer

Dramaline Publications

Dramaline Publications
36-851 Palm View Road
Rancho Mirage, CA 92270
Phone 619/770-6076 Fax 619/770-4507

Library of Congress Cataloging-in-Publication Data

Speeches and Scenes from Oscar's Best Films, edited by Dick Dotterer
        p.   cm.
   Includes index.
   ISBN 0-940669-26-9: $19.95
   1. Motion Pictures—Quotations, maxims, etc.
   2. Academy Awards (Motion pictures) I. Dotterer, Dick.
PN1994.9.S66   1994
791.43'75—dc20   94-15296

Cover art by John Sabel

ACKNOWLEDGEMENTS

The editor would like to thank the librarians and staff of the Library of the Academy of Motion Picture Arts and Sciences where the majority of this book was researched and all of the manuscripts used as source material for this book are housed. The library is becoming a major resource and repository for film memorabilia and historical archives for the art and crafts of film-making.

The editor would also like to thank Mary Lu Wehmeier of Pixel Perfect Systems for her help in realizing this book from the mysteries and complications of computer systems, and Dan Fendel, who also helped with the rituals of computer mysteries.

The publisher would like to thank David Payne and Deb Murphy of Turner Entertainment for their cooperation in making this book possible.

CONTENTS

SCENES CLASSIFIED BY NUMBER OF CHARACTERS

All of the films in this collection are available on video cassette, and all but two—*Cimarron*, and *The Life of Emile Zola*—are available on laserdisc.

The speech and scene breakdown for each film is as follows:

ONE MALE:
Cimarron—1
Grand Hotel—2
Mutiny on the Bounty—1
The Life of Emile Zola—3

ONE FEMALE:
Cimarron—1

ONE MALE/ONE FEMALE:
Cimarron—1
Grand Hotel—2
The Great Ziegfeld—3
The Life of Emile Zola—2
Mrs. Miniver—1
An American in Paris—2
Ben Hur—1

TWO MALE:
Mutiny on the Bounty—1
Gigi—1
Ben Hur—2

TWO FEMALE:
Grand Hotel—1
The Great Ziegfeld—1
Mrs. Miniver—2
Gigi—1

ONE MALE/TWO FEMALE:
The Great Ziegfelfd—1
Gigi—1

TWO MALE/ ONE FEMALE:
The Great Ziegfelfd—1
Mrs. Miniver—1
An American in Paris—2

TWO MALE/TWO FEMALE:
The Great Ziegfeld—1

PREFACE

BE AN APPLE

I always look for the actor with personality first. I've found that a person with a fantastic personality will attract the attention of everyone in the room, not unlike a beautiful young woman. But people will look at the beauty and after a moment return to their conversation. The one with the personality will hold their attention.

AL TRESCONY
Principal talent scout for M-G-M

When I directed an interview test, I would go to a head close-up and watch the eyes, because the eyes show everything the person is thinking. It comes through the celluloid right out to the audience.

SOLLY BAIAN
Principal talent scout for Warner Brothers

In motion pictures there is a camera, what I have termed a truth machine. *You cannot say* dog *and think* cat, *because* meow *will come out if you do.*

LILLIAN BURNS
Head of M-G-M talent department and principal M-G-M acting coach

I think it's possible to teach the craft and art of acting, especially film acting. There are a lot of craft things to learn. Certainly the development of a persona becomes part of that, helping young people open up and have presence and vitality, the energy, the magic. But filming a long shot is one kind of communication; when they pull in for a tight close-up, it really has to stay just in the eyes. The smallest mannerism is five-feet big. If you move your mouth a little, that's five-feet of movement. So that communication is different.

ESTELLE HARMAN
Talent coordinator and acting coach for Universal

The story goes something like this: When Carol Bruce was a young contract player at Universal Studios part of her obligation to the studio was—as with all novice contract players—to take acting lessons from coaches provided by the studio. Carol Bruce, who became a dependable Broadway actress, drew classes taught by the distinguished Russian *émigré* actress, Maria Ouspenskaya. "Madame" or "Madame Ouspenskaya," as she preferred to be addressed, had been both a student and colleague of

Konstantin Stanislavski at the Moscow Art Theater before she immigrated to the United States in the 1930s.

Madame was more than an acting coach on the Universal lot, of course. She was a respected actress, having twice been nominated for he Academy Award (for *Dodsworth* in 1937, and *Love Affair*, 1939). Madame was a tiny dynamo of a woman who always wore high heels so as to be as tall as possible. But as an actress and a teacher she easily touched the stars. However, Madame was often awesome and intimidating to the young novice who was uninitiated to her ways. (Madame died tragically in 1949, the result of a fire in her apartment.)

Carol Bruce was one of the uninitiated, but also one who found the experience of working with Maria Ouspenskaya inspiring. Miss Bruce was enchanted and mesmerized by the dynamics and dimensions of Madame's personality and her classes. Upon their first meeting Madame commanded Carol Bruce to be an apple. The beginning actress was puzzled. She couldn't envision what she was supposed to do. With a certain amount of sudden inspiration, brought on, no doubt, by a dollop of panic and desperation, Miss Bruce puffed out her cheeks to make her face round, while at the same time making a face and holding her breath. "Magnificent!" cried Madame Ouspenskaya. "Wonderful. You have imagination."

You see, when Hollywood and moviemaking were centered in a massive studio system and the destiny of actors' careers (and, indeed, their very lives) were controlled by a handful of "tyrannical" moguls, the studios and their bosses put inexperienced contract players into extensive apprentice programs. These programs were designed to groom the young actor for a future career and future stardom. In other words, while the contract player was being paid a salary by the studio, the studio took the trouble to invest in the young novice actor's potential, to teach him or her how to master the craft of film-making, to help him or her become an accomplished film actor, director, or whatever the future might hold.

This apprentice program was an elaborate one. It was a financial gamble by the studio on the future of the young contract player, which the studio hoped would turn into a profitable investment. The apprentice program was designed not only to teach the craft of film-making, it also taught young actors about grooming, how to conduct themselves, how to dress, about music, aspects of culture, how to sit—even how to hold a glass if need be.

Lillian Burns, the legendary head of the talent department at M-G-M and that studio's leading drama coach, believed in the development of the total persona. She believed that if you developed the total person, you developed the talent. "I don't believe you can teach acting," she said. "You can teach voice, you can teach diction, you can teach body movement. You can help develop talent, or even a great personality. That's where the big studios could make stars."

While encouraged by Louis B. Mayer to produce stage plays on the Metro lot, Burns refused to do so. She believed that stage acting was at odds with film acting. But every Friday groups of young players would gather in her office area to perform for each other scenes from movies they were currently shooting, or scenes from older scripts. Burns' goals for the fledgling actors were simple and straightforward. She wanted the apprentice to understand the script and the character. She wanted actors to sharpen their tools, to let go of their inhibitions. She admonished her charges never to try to "act" but to be honest and simple. She urged them and tried to teach them to project from the eyes instead of just with the voice. But above all, she insisted that each be an individual and not copy another's interpretation.

Phyllis Loughton, head of talent at Paramount, had a different philosophy and approach. She had previously been at Metro, before moving to Paramount, and while at Metro had presented stage plays with new actors. She continued to do so at Paramount. Three times a year she presented plays and invited producers and directors to see the work of the new contract players. While she agreed that there was a difference between stage acting and film acting, Loughton believed that young players needed to learn to use their voices, their bodies, and how to be characters other than themselves. Stage plays provided these opportunities for the young actor to stretch and grow. (Phyllis Loughton was cagey enough to realize that a dynamic personality, fascinating looks, and a good voice could compensate for the lack of acting ability on film.)

Whatever the philosophy, whether acting could be taught of if it was the total persona that made the actor, all of the studios were in agreement that the new players had to learn a different technique for film-making from straight stage acting. And each offered their contract players lessons in speech, voice and diction, singing, dance, horseback riding, fencing, boxing, movement, swimming, etiquette, foreign languages—whatever was needed for the motion pictures.

The actors also learned how to care for their bodies and their clothes. They learned how to perform positively at an interview, how to appear in public. They were given exercise classes, were offered guest lectures on a wide range of subjects, were taught aspects of make-up and skin care. Some studios even had barber shops and dentists on the lot. (The dentists not only cleaned teeth, they also capped them—free.) While most of the lessons were optional, the ambitious players took advantage of these gift horses. A great many of the more ambitious young players, who later established themselves in long careers in film, spent four or five hours a day, six days a week, in classes when they weren't in front of the cameras.

Ambitious and astute young actors realized that they were being given an opportunity to train and develop into a versatile performers, qualified professionals. And they were being *paid* for the opportunity. The bright ones took maximum advantage of the situation.

Even though the competition was brutal, even though the studios demanded long hours and controlled image making, they were also instrumental in nurturing and seasoning the young and inexperienced. They gambled on the future of these young actors because these actors' futures were also the studios'.

We don't have the big studio support systems anymore. Today, in the time of the independent production companies and independent producers, within the small studio, which is little more than a rented sound stage, we do not have elaborate apprentice programs. Today, such programs have been relegated to high school courses, to college and university radio/TV/film departments (departments of communications), and to various other professional training schools and programs—and private teachers. Today, rather than having an elaborate set of goals and courses planned for them, or have a schedule of events designed to enhance their development, novice film actors have to create their own apprentice programs. They have to plan, stick with, and finance their own agendas, and employ their diligence and integrity in order to master their craft.

One of the purposes of this book is offer the actor/director/writer a ready reference from pictures that have made film history. This book is *not* about how to act in a film, nor how to direct one, or write a screenplay. This compendium of speeches and scenes is for the enlightenment of actors, directors, writers, art directors, cinematographers—practitioners of filmmaking at all levels. It is meant to be a rich, inspirational resource. It may also prove of interest to the film-buff, movie-goer, TV viewer, or anyone interested in a hands-on reference to some the greatest movies ever made.

This book is limited in scope by the very screenplays and the time period from which they were chosen. Each won the Academy Award for Best Picture for its respective year.

These films are products of the major studios during the heyday of the studio system. And are the result of the nurturing studio system. And the screenplays presented herein are representational of the best and most varied screenwriting of the period. And the scripts are penned by some of the most distinguished writers of the time.

For many years, it has been fashionable to support the idea that the screenwriter doesn't write the movie—that it is the director who takes a raw idea and renders it meaningful. It has also been said that the hallmark of a great screenplay is the absence of language and the presence of an abundance of car crashes, explosions, and special effects. This is not necessarily true.

Since people talk, films about people require dialogue. However, when a writer creates a believable character—one the actor can breathe life into, a character that lives in a believable world—it is possible to eliminate dialogue and translate ideas into actions.

Film characters are defined by what they say, what they do, where they go, and what they see. A film, obviously, is a visual medium. The visual (the camera) is used to replace words. Words are replaced by various locations (rather than descriptions), rapid manipulation and changes of space, perspectives, and points of view. The screenwriter tends to write in simple, everyday speech rather than in metaphors or rhetoric images because the camera communicates image.

The camera captures the character's naturalistic behavior and delineates characterization by capturing the smallest actions and movements. (A written note, or a close-up of a bottle of pills can reveal more quickly to the audience the state of emotional balance of a character than three minutes of dialogue.) Film allows the actor communicate a powerful performance with a minimum of motion. (The more the actor understands this—that less is more—the greater the artistic freedom.)

The screenplay provides a great deal of support for the film actor. It is more than a matter of lights, costume, make-up—even dialogue. Cuts and intercuts to other actors' responses while one actor is speaking greatly affects audience reaction. The actor also receives support from controlled visual scenes and scene composition.

Great film-making is not the absence of language. Language—words, dialogue—is still a major tool of the actor. However, it is the creative use of the visual medium to express ideas, expound actions, and express emotion that produces exemplary movies. The point is not to eliminate dialogue. But in film the reliance is not upon words to express ideas and feelings.

Just as the playwright and screenwriter must employ different techniques, the actor must also make adjustments to accommodate the different mediums. It is a matter of environment and mechanics dictating method, and acting well in one medium does not assure success in the other. The actor must master the techniques of both stage and film and utilize the nuances of each in the realization of a competent performance. Stage actors must reach out from themselves. They must project. They must communicate to every corner of the theater. Film actors, on the other hand, are required to draw themselves inward, minimize, and pull the audience into the performance. Each technique is specific and each is valid. But whether on state or screen, it is the actor's obligation to communicate with the audience, to create a believable character, to give an individual, original, honest performance.

THE EDITOR

INTRODUCTION

All of the selections found in this book have been taken from manuscripts of the shooting scripts of the film plays. In those cases where two or more versions of the script existed in manuscript form, the one closest to the actual shooting script was chosen.

Also, in some cases, some of the speeches and scenes chosen will not be found in the released film, even though they are taken from the approved shooting script. For example: In *Mrs. Miniver*, the scene between Mrs. Miniver and the fugitive German flier has a few lines between Mrs. Miniver and the milkman. In the film, however, the milkman remains a background character outside the house. His milk bottles are heard clanking, but his form remains a blur that passes by the curtains of the kitchen window.

This book is a workshop library for the discovery of the uniqueness of interpretation on the part of the performer. It is not for the purpose of aping another actor's work. The memorable actor is a unique, fascinating, individual personality. The characters are open to a wide variety of interpretations. And here I state the obvious: There was only one Garbo, Gable, Leigh, Bogart, and Hepburn, and the characters they portrayed were created by writers to be interpreted—believably—in relation to the core of the character and the story's intent.

The scenes in this book are reproduced, without alteration, from authentic sources. This was done in the interest of supplying actors, directors, film buffs—anyone interested in the great films of the period—with an original source of reference.

REGARDING THE EDITOR

Dick Dotterer holds an M.F.A. in playwriting and directing. He is a published playwright and author. He has also worked as a dramaturg and literary manager; and has worked in educational theater, taught acting, and guest lectured on playwriting and directing. He currently resides in Los Angeles, California.

CIMARRON

Cimarron means: wild, bad, unruly. . . . It is the name of a man, a
river, a country, a novel, and now a picture.

STUDIO ADVERTISING

RKO RADIO 1930–31
Produced by William LeBaron
Directed by Wesley Ruggles
Screenplay by Howard Estabrook
From the novel of the same name by Edna Ferber

AAN: Best picture, Actor (Richard Dix), Actress
(Irene Dunn), Director, Screenplay (adaptation),
Cinematography, Interior decoration

Picture, Screenplay, Interior decoration

CAST
Richard Dix, Irene Dunne, Estelle Taylor, Nance O'Neill,
William Collier, Jr., Roscoe Ates, George E. Stone,
Stanley Fields, Edna May Oliver

Seen today, one wonders what all the brouhaha was about over this creaky epic. It is melodramatic and laughable in many of its performances by to-day's standards. Richard Dix was a silent screen star who excelled in rugged, outdoor adventures. This film was to mark his major transition into sound pictures. His performance is exaggerated and non-believable, but he *was* nominated as Best Actor of the Year! Only the performances of Edna May Oliver, an extremely gifted comedic character actress with the face of a plug horse, and the performance of Irene Dunne, which hints at the Irene Dunne who was to flower into one of the most gifted of American film actresses, are memorable today. Whatever was the Academy thinking when they gave *this* film their treasured statuette? Surely one of the contenders, the classic first version of *The Front Page*, for example—which still holds interest and admiration today—would have been a better choice.

Cimarron was certainly a spectacle, and a spectacle with *sound*. The enormous panorama of the Oklahoma land rush far exceeded any previous attempts made by sound pictures. It had a cast of thousands—literally, including an entire Osage tribe to play "authentic" Indians. Several different versions of the principal town had to be built to accommodate the changes of the land, the people, and the background over the forty-year time span of the film's story. It cost a record $1.4 million dollars to make—and lost $565,000. But it brought enormous prestige to RKO Radio Pictures. It also gathered seven nominations in a competition that had only nine categories.

Cimarron was the first Western to win the Academy Award as Best Picture. In fact, it was the *only* Western to be so named until it was joined by *Dances with Wolves* (1990) and *The Unforgiven* (1992). The movie is based on another of those sprawling, generational novels by Edna Ferber. *Cimarron* concerns Yancy and Sabra Cravat and their offsprings. Yancy is a pioneer— he was born under a wandering star. He is *always* looking for a new adventure.

Yancy has married the devoted Sabra. Devoted she may be, but she thinks of herself as a rooted tree rather than a tumbleweed. Yancy and Sabra help settle the Indian Territory (Oklahoma) by participating in the land rush. They also establish a successful newspaper and homestead some land. Then Yancy gets the wanderlust again. Finally, he disappears over the horizon for good, leaving the raising of his family and the operation of the newspaper to his wife. But Sabra is a "Ferber woman" who can handle all crises. Sabra soon becomes as much a part of the Oklahoma landscape as the red clay. Her stature is such that she is chosen as the state's first congressional representative, She is also a humanist and proves it when she supports her son Cimarron's marriage to the daughter of an Osage Indian chief. (Keep in mind: This was written and filmed at a time when such unions carried serious social consequences.) Irene Dunne raises feminine heroism to the heights of Lillian Gish.

SABRA and YANCY

Yancy Cravat (Dix) is both charming and irresponsible. He is one of the breed of "pioneers" who kept looking for the next adventure over the horizon. As a result, during the course of the story he shifts his journalistic and political duties to his wife, Sabra (Dunne), who is a classic Edna Ferber heroine.

Yancy and Sabra have become "established" in town for one of the longest periods in Yancy's life. He is the editor of the local newspaper. But he's getting anxious to move on, to find the next adventure, the next new challenge to conquer. In this case it's the land rush authorized by Grover Cleveland in the Oklahoma Territory. Sabra, while she loves her husband, does not necessarily agree with his proclivity of always wanting to see what's beyond the horizon. Their present home and hearth is quite enough for her.

INT. OFFICE—DAY

Yancy is at the desk, telegram set before him. He is starting to write an article. He glances intermittently at the telegram as he writes. During this—overlap action—SOUND: (OFF STAGE) Chatter of women. Side door closes. Chatter stops. After moment, Sabra enters, flushed with her social triumph. Yancy's back is toward her.

SABRA

(Stimulated with her first public success.)
Darling! The whole membership turned out to
hear my address! It's wonderful!—the way
the women are getting together! *(Hands on his
shoulders.)* You're right, dear. I do like it here,
after all! *(Affectionate pressure.)* I'm glad we
came away from Wichita! *(Fondles him a
moment, then brightly backs away, displays her
dress.)* And you should have seen them open
their eyes at this! *(Proudly adjusts her sleeve.)*
What do you think of it? *(Displays gown, poses
expectantly for his approval.)*

YANCY

(Surveys her—dryly.) Cruelty to animals.

SABRA

*(Attractively chiding him. Superior feminine
wisdom.)* It's the very latest thing from Chicago.

YANCY

When some of those old squaws see it, they'll
get a pair, and carry a papoose in each sleeve.

SABRA

(Knowingly.) Cousin Bella writes they'll be even
larger by autumn.

Yancy smiles whimsically. He takes up the telegram and glances at it.

YANCY

(Far away mood.) By autumn. . . .

SABRA

(*Repressed intuitive apprehension.*) What's in
the telegram?

YANCY

News, Sugar. Proclamation by President
Cleveland setting September 16 for the opening
of the Cherokee Strip.

SABRA

(*Understandingly.*) The Cherokee land?

YANCY

Government has brought it from the Indians—
for the huge sum—a dollar forty an acre—
pushing them farther back.

SABRA

(*Knowingly.*) A good thing. They made no use
of it.

YANCY

(*Affectionately.*) Honey!— Come here!

Arrested by his vivid tone, she comes to him.

CUT TO:

INT. OFFICE—DAY—(INTERCUT SEVERAL ANGLES)—CLOSER
VIEW

YANCY

(*With vision.*) A new run! The biggest thing yet!
Three times more land than in '89!

SABRA

(*Quick, tremulous, vague fear.*) What of it?

YANCY

(*Swinging on.*) Another new wilderness to
become livable territory—

SABRA

(*Sharp alarm.*) You don't mean?—

YANCY

(*Dynamic.*) Let's go, Sabra! Get an allotment of
that Cherokee land!—

SABRA

(*Stunned.*) Leave here?

YANCY

Sell out the paper at a profit! Go for a townsite!

SABRA

(*Appalled.*) Give up all we've worked and slaved
for—(*piteously.*)

YANCY

We left Wichita—escaped being smothered in
advice and Southern fried chicken!— Let's get
out of all of this. . . . (*Pushes marshmallow salad
away.*)

SABRA

(*Suffering.*) Oh—was Mother right!—when she
said you'd go for the adventure of it.
(*Memories.*) Five years—the longest time
you've ever spent in one place—and you've
been here only four!

YANCY

It's a new empire, Sabra! We'll see it grow
before our eyes into a new state!

SABRA

(*Suffering.*) We can't tear up our lives and start
over again. You've done your share! Let the
others go! . . .

YANCY

(*Looking intently.*) Sabra . . . (*Doesn't want to hurt her.*) I'll send back for you.

SABRA

(*Knows he's going.*) Oh—my boy!— (*Affectionately.*) Let's not talk any more about it! (*Puts an arm around him—thinks he is persuaded. Yancy kisses her—deep in thought. Turns away.*)

CUT TO:

INT. OFFICE—DAY—FRESH ANGLE

Yancy turns away from Sabra.

YANCY

(*Hums vaguely.*) Hi rickety whoop ti do—How I love to sing to you—(*Crossing to small cabinet. Opens door.*)

CUT TO:

INT. OFFICE. DAY—CLOSE VIEW—YANCY AT CABINET

Yancy is opening the cabinet door. He takes out his saddlebags, which are already packed, and his gun belt.

YANCY

(*Continues humming.*)

CUT TO:

INT. OFFICE—DAY—FRESH ANGLE—VIEW TOWARD
WINDOW AND STREET

Sabra sees a cavalcade of twenty horsemen riding up in the street, leading an extra horse with empty saddle, obviously for Yancy. As Sabra spies this horse, the truth crashes in upon her.

SABRA

(*Piteously.*) You're not leaving—now—
today?—

In the street a group of horsemen yell louder: Yip! Yip! Y-e-o-w! Firing six shooters. SOUND: Shots of revolvers. Yancy straps on his gun belt.

SABRA

(*Frightened.*) You can't go—like this!—

YANCY

(*Tenderly.*) Sugar!— (*Realizing the fact that makes them different.*)

SABRA

(*Clutches him. Clings to him with love.*) I can't
let you go!—

YANCY

(*Hotly.*) Go with me!

SABRA

(*Half hysterical.*) The children! . . .

YANCY

The children, too—all of us!—now!

SABRA

(*Anguished finality.*) We can't!—(*Piteous,
pleading.*) Don't go! Don't go!

YANCY

I've got to go!

He pulls away from Sabra and leaves.

SABRA

Years ago, Sabra lost her fight with Yancy for a stable, family existence. In fact, Yancy went riding off into the sunset and out of Sabra's and his children's lives. But Sabra is a woman created by Edna Ferber and she is resourceful and resilient. Sabra took over those projects and duties that Yancy cavalierly left behind. Sabra became editor and publisher of the newspaper and raised it in stature. Finally, after several years, Sabra is rewarded by the state she helped to settle and establish by being the first woman elected to Congress. She is now fifty-seven, and even though she has neither seen nor known the whereabouts of her husband for years, she pretends that he is simply out of town on business. She is so respected by the township that they openly agree to agree with her self-ruse.

SABRA

(*With feeling.*) My friends . . . Today I stand before you with a new responsibility. Time has passed for many of us, since we first met in the early days of Osage . . . time, that mellows our hearts and tells us all the truth. To many others among you, including our distinguished guests from Washington, I appear more or less a stranger. I want you all to know me and mine as we are—to meet my family as if you were in my home. . . . (*Affectionately.*) First, my youngest— my daughter Donna (*Gestures toward Donna, out of scene—spirited, tender charm.*) Stand up, dear, and let them see you! Next, my first born—(*Warmly.*)—my boy, Cimarron— (*Gestures toward Cim, out of scene.*) (*She summons up her subtle reserves, determined to make her next point tell heavily. Impressively.*) And now, one who has become a member of our family by marriage—(*Veiled defiance.*) My son's wife, a Chief's daughter—("I dare you" spirit.)—a full-blooded Osage Indian, Ruby Big Elk—Mrs. Cimarron Cravat! (*Sound O.S., great applause.*) And my grandchildren—Felice and— (*Touch of feeling as she speaks name.*) Yancy— Second. (*Tenderly—controlling her emotion.*) I am sorry—this afternoon—that I cannot call upon— (*A moment—deep feeling.*)—my husband. . . . (*Pauses.*)—but he is out of the city.

I know he would be glad to be here and greet you. . . . (*Her voice breaks.*) (*A firm tone—over her feelings.*) As for myself—I can only thank you for the office you have conferred upon me. . . . The women of Oklahoma—have helped build a prairie wilderness into the state of today! . . . The holding of a public office by a woman is a natural step. I pledge to you that I will do my best. (*She sits down.*)

GRAND HOTEL

If Crawford provides the film with its melodrama, Garbo endows it with its magic.

M-G-M 1931–32
Produced by Irving Thalberg
Directed by Edmund Goulding
Screenplay by William A. Drake
From the novel and stage play of the same name by Vicki Baum

AAN: Best Picture

AA: Best Picture

CAST
Greta Garbo, John Barrymore, Lionel Barrymore, Joan Crawford,
Wallace Beery, Jean Hersholt, Lewis Stone

There were eight pictures nominated for Best Picture in the 1931–32 competition. Of that number, four had only one nomination, for Best Picture, *Grand Hotel* among them. With a stellar cast that included Garbo, John and Lionel Barrymore, Wallace Beery, an affecting Joan Crawford, stalwart Lewis Stone, and dependable Jean Hersholt, and a series of sets that were so shiny that 200 pairs of woolen socks were worn out daily by the cast and crew to keep the polished surface of the floors from being scuffed and to keep the noise down. At times there were as many as six cameras shooting a single sequence, breaking up into different cuts that were planned in advance. It is still a wonder today that the Academy did not take notice of a number of other qualities of the film.

Vicki Baum worked as a chambermaid to gather material for her internationally acclaimed novel. Then she adapted it into a stage play which became an international hit, playing in Berlin, Paris, Vienna, London, Rome, New York, Chicago, San Francisco, and Los Angeles. But none of the stage productions, however, ever assumed the importance of the film version with its unique, all-star cast. (The story was refilmed in 1945. This time setting the action in a grand hotel in New York City. The remake was entitled *Weekend at the Waldorf.*)

This is the first film in which Greta Garbo was billed simply as "Garbo." It was also the film in which she uttered her now famous signature line "I want to be alone." *Grand Hotel* is one of the first examples of M-G-M's glittering motion picture extravaganzas, for which it became quickly known, and of which this studio became the leading producer.

The action of *Grand Hotel* occurs in a twenty-four hour period and intertwines the lives of a series of disparate people, from the reclusive, depressed prima ballerina Grusinskaya (Garbo), to a poor factory clerk Kringelein (Lionel Barrymore) who is dying and has decided to have his last fling, to a dissolute aristocrat The Baron (John Barrymore) who has resorted to theft to pay his debts, to a thuggish factory owner Preysing (Berry), to a timid stenographer Flaemmchen (Crawford). In the grandest, most expensive hotel in post-WWI Berlin, in its most decadent period, they come as strangers to each other, and affect the lives and futures of each.

PREYSING

Both the film and the stage play open with a tried-and-true method of presenting expository material—a telephone conversation. In this case it works. It also establishes the hectic atmosphere of the hotel, as well as introducing the characters to the audience individually, proceeding to convey their interactions.

Preysing is the owner/manager of a factory in another part of Germany. He has arrived in Berlin, a man desperate to make a business merger work out. If he does not, he faces financial ruin, and financial ruin to him is total ruin. Preysing is a petty tyrant as a factory owner and manager. But he is an impartial petty tyrant: he treats all people with equal disdain. Anyone who comes within his sphere has but one purpose in life, to serve him.

IN A TELEPHONE BOOTH IN THE LOBBY OF THE GRAND HOTEL— BERLIN

PREYSING

Hello! Long distance? . . . Get off the wire. . . .
No. . . . I was talking to Fredersdorf. . . . What?
. . . Oh, hello! . . . Is that you dear? . . . How is
everything at home? . . . What do you hear from
the factory? . . . No. . . . How are the children?
. . . I left my shaving set at home. . . . Yes, is
your father there? . . . Hello, Father? . . . Our
stock has gone down twenty-three points. If our
merger with Saxonia doesn't go through—I
don't know what we can do. . . . Hello, hello. . . .

Yes, Papa. Rely on me—everything depends on
Manchester. . . . If they refuse to come in—well,
we will be in bad shape. . . . No. . . . Rely on me,
I'll make it go through—I'll make it go through.
. . . Waiting? . . . Yes, I'm still speaking—

CAMERA PANS to the next booth:

KRINGELEIN

Kringelein has probably spent his entire adult working life in servile positions to his employer, Preysing and Company. Kringelein has never been
anything but an insignificant clerk in the factory, and he has accepted himself
as an insignificant human being on the face of the planet. But now he has
found that he is dying and the diagnosis is non-reversible. As a result, he has
decided to cash in all his savings and go out in the manner and style he has
seen others do and has dreamed about. He is going to spend his money on
one last fling in the grandest, most enchanting place he can think of. He's
chosen the Grand Hotel. Given Kringelein's background and the character
evolved from it, this is a very courageous and adventurous road for him to
travel.

LOBBY PHONE BOOTH IN THE GRAND HOTEL—BERLIN

KRINGELEIN
Who is that? This is. . . . Hello, hello! . . . Who is
that. . . . Heinrich? This is Kringelein. Hello,
Heinrich. This is Otto Kringelein. Hello! Can
you hear me? . . . I've got to speak very quickly.
Every minute costs two marks ninety. . . . What?
. . . Otto Kringelein! Yes, I'm in Berlin, staying
at the best hotel, the Grand Hotel. . . . No, don't
you understand? I want to explain, but I must do
so quickly, it costs so much. Please don't
interrupt me—Hello? Hello! Listen! You know
that will I made before my operation? I gave it to
you. I want you to tear it up. Destroy it. Because,
listen, I came to Berlin to see a great specialist
about that old trouble of mine. . . . It's pretty
bad, Heinrich. The specialist says I can't live
much longer. (*Louder.*) I haven't long to live!

That's what's the matter! Hello, hello. Are you
on the line? No, it isn't nice to be told a thing
like that. All sorts of things run through your
head. I am going to stay here in Berlin. I am
never coming back to Fredersdorf. Never! I want
to get something out of life, too. You plague,
and bother, and save—and all of a sudden you
are dead. Heinrich. . . . You don't say anything. I
am in the Grand Hotel, do you understand, the
most expensive hotel in Berlin? I'm going to get
a room here. The very best people stay here. Our
big boss, Preysing, too. I saw him—not five
minutes after I was here. Sometime I'd like to
tell him exactly what I think of him. Listen,
Henrich—I have taken all my savings; my life
insurance, too; I cashed in all my policies, the
sick benefit fund, the old-age pension, the
unemployment insurance, the burial fund and
everything. . . . What's that, miss? . . . Hello,
Henrich. I have to hang—up now. I have to pay
three times overcharge. Just think Heinrich!
There's music here all day long. And in the
evening, they go round in full dress. . . . Yes,
sometimes I have pain, but I can stand it.
Everything is frightfully expensive here. You
can imagine, the Grand Hotel. . . . What? Time's
up. I'm a sick man—Heinrich—Hello—Hello—
Operator—Every minute two marks
ninety. . . . *(He hangs up.)*

GRUSINSKAYA and SUZETTE

Grusinskaya is an internationally known prima ballerina. She is also an unhappy and empty woman, slightly melancholy by the present circumstances
of her life, but she is not sure why all of this is to be so, and she continually
searches for the cause—or for the blame. She is treated special, so therefore
she thinks that as a person, not simply as a ballerina, she *is* special.
Grusinskaya has reached a very selfish point in her life: Rather than think
about her responsiblity to her public, to the members of the ballet company,
to her art, Grusinskaya has neared the point of the stereotypical "artiste" who
thinks only of herself and hides behind temperment and "I don't feel like it."
What keeps Gruinskaya from being a complete bore is that she is a woman

with some really serious emotional darkness: The woman is at a crisis in her
career, her life, and her soul. And she doesn't know how to handle it or what
to do; she just knows that she must do something for she is too unhappy to
remain where she is. It is simply too painful.

It is nearing the time when Grusinskaya must go to the theater to prepare
for the performance that night. She has been sleeping, resting for the performance, and her loyal and conscientious maid, Suzette, has been trying to
make life for her mistress as pleasant as possible.

GRUSINSKAYA'S ROOM

*It is typical hotel. Half-open trunks, etc. Curtains are drawn—the room is
in semi-darkness. There is a sense of silence, except for distant music
coming from the Yellow Room below. In Suzette's hands we see one of
Grusiinskaya's ballet slippers, which she has been mending. She is about to
tiptoe to her seat when she stops suddenly and looks off dramatically at . . .*

GRUSINSKAYA—SHOT FROM HER ANGLE

*She is sleeping beneath a Chinese robe, on the chaise lounge. Apparently
she has changed her position, because the hand that is outside the robe
moves. The CAMERA, as though it were Suzette, MOVES UP towards
Grusinskaya. Her eyes are closed. Suzette crosses to the chaise lounge and is
looking down. Grusinskaya's eyes open suddenly. She looks at the ceiling
and then her eyes turn and look straight at Suzette.*

> **SUZETTE'S VOICE**
> (*Quietly and reverently—almost a whisper.*)
> Madam has slept well.

> **GRUSINSKAYA**
> No, I have been awake—thinking—thinking.

> **SUZETTE'S VOICE**
> It is time for the performance.

> **GRUSINSKAYA**
> The performance?

SUZETTE

It is time.

GRUSINSKAYA

(*Like a soldier called to attention Grusinskaya sits suddenly upright.*) Always the performance—every day the performance—time of the performance. (*She pauses and droops suddenly.*) I think, Suzette, I have never been so tired in my life. (*She takes the bottle of veronal which is nearby.*) Veronal didn't even help me to sleep. (*Laughs a little.*)

SUZETTE

(*Speaking into the telephone.*) Madam Grusinskaya's car is to be brought.

While she is speaking Grusinskaya rises—with the grace of a dancer she picks up the Chinese robe that has fallen to the floor, and although there is only one other woman in the room—she holds the robe around her. She crosses to the mirror and looks at her face, running her fingers through her hair. She gently massages under her eyes and the CAMERA sees Grusinskaya for the first time. There is a silence in the room—neither of the women speak. Suzette gets madam's clothes ready. She crosses, puts the case of pearls down on the dressing table and opens them. Grusinskaya looks into space—silence—dead silence. Suzette kneels as if to put madam's stockings on for her. Grusinskaya pulls her foot away.

GRUSINSKAYA

I can't dance tonight—

SUZETTE

It will pass—it will pass—come.

GRUSINSKAYA

Let us cancel the engagement.

SUZETTE

But Madam cannot do that.

GRUSINSKAYA

Now is the time to cancel, to stop entirely.
I feel it—everything tells me—enough—
enough. (*She leans forward against the dressing
table and her hands unconsciously touch the
pearls. Very quietly:*) The pearls are cold—
everything is cold—finished—it seems so far
away—so threadbare—the Russians—
St. Petersburg—the Imperial Court—the Grand
Duke Sergei—(*Long pause as though she were
reliving incidents of the past.*) —Sergei—dead—
Grusinskaya—it's all gone. (*She throws the
pearls away, down upon the floor.*)

SUZETTE

Mon Dieu—the pearls—if they were to break—

GRUSINSKAYA

The pearls won't break—they hold together and
bring me bad luck—I hate them!

SUZETTE

(*She crosses replacing the pearls.*) Orchids
come again, Madam—no card—I think perhaps
they are from the same young man—he is at the
end of the corridor—tall—he walks like a
soldier—Madam must have noticed how often
he is in the elevator with us. Last night for
instance—

GRUSINSKAYA

Oh, Suzette—Suzette— Shh—quiet.
(*Grusinskaya's eyes are looking off into space—
she is away in Russia—she does not look—
Telephone rings—Suzette crosses to telephone.*)

SUZETTE

Ah, oui—the car is here for Madam.

GRUSINSKAYA

Send it away—I shan't need it. (*There is a knock
at the door—a certain kind of knock.*) Come in.
(*She picks up the telephone and as she does so
Pimenov enters. Suzette quickly gives Pimenov a
signal that there is trouble. As Pimenov is
closing the door we hear Grusinskaya speak into
the telephone. Authoritatively:*) Madam
Grusinskaya will not require her car—no—she
will not be going to the theater.

GRUSINSKAYA and THE BARON

Here it is, folks, the scene in which Garbo pronounced those famous words "I
want to be alone." Actually, she says it not once, but twice. And she doesn't
say it to the press (as many suppose); she says it to John Barrymore.

Things have not been going well for either the Baron or Grusinskaya in
their lives. The Baron is a handsome, dashing, charming, romantic figure of a
financially destitute aristocrat. He is in such desperate need for money that he
sees no other way to alleviate this problem except to turn to a life of crime—
stealing a very valuable string of pearls that belongs to Grusinskaya.
(Remember how they were emphasized in the preceeding scene?)

Grusinskaya is supposed to be at the theater, ready to perform. She
balked at performing and came back to the hotel. The Baron has managed to
break into Grusinskaya's empty suite, but before he can make his exit with
the pearls, the ballerina and her entourage arrive. The Baron has to hide
behind a set of convenient drapes by the windows (Shakespeare had his arras,
the movies have their window drapes.) Grusinskaya manages to dismiss her
companions, and all the Baron has to do is wait for his chance to escape the
suite.

GRUSINSKAYA'S HOTEL ROOM—NIGHT

*Suzette and Meierheim have just left—been thrown out by Grusinskaya. She
is alone in the room.*

NOTE (FROM THE SCREENPLAY): DURING THIS SCENE, INTERCUT ʹ
SHOTS OF BARON

*It is some time before Grusinskaya moves. She crosses to door—turns the
key—takes the key out of the lock and throws it away—from her—out upon
the floor. She crosses slowly to the mirror, regards herself, silently. We hear
the strains from Preysing's radio playing a light Viennese waltz.
Grusinskaya begins suddenly to sob.*

FLASH OF BARON—WATCHING HER

GRUSINSKAYA

*Quite suddenly—as if with resolution she begins to undress. Then she
becomes weary again. With a garment in her hand, she moves slowly toward
the curtain—where the Baron is standing.*

BARON

We see him grow tense.

GRUSINSKAYA

She drops the garment listlessly to the floor—moves out of scene.

CLOSE-UP OF BARON

He peeps around the curtains.

CUT TO:

GRUSINSKAYA

*She is in a thin robe. She sits before mirror—looks steadily at her face. Her
head goes down suddenly in her hands and we hear her say:*

GRUSINSKAYA
The end—over—finished— (*Suddenly she
moves quickly across the room. Goes to
bathroom.*)

Baron half starts out toward door. He watches—darts across the room as if towards the door. He hears her coming and darts quickly into the half- open door of the closet. She re-enters—carrying a glass of water. She crosses, places the glass down beside the bed—her movements are quick and furtive— then she crosses, picks up the telephone—asks for the theater.

GRUSINSKAYA

The Western Theater—

She leaves receiver down—crosses quickly to mirror—stands there and brushes back her hair—crosses back to telephone; speaks:

GRUSINSKAYA

Western Theater? (*She glances up at the clock.*) The stage—Mr. Pimonev—the ballet master— Grusinskaya—hurry—hurry. (*Again she puts receiver down—picking up a pencil she commences hastily to scribble a note. She writes frantically. Her other hand goes up and picks up the receiver.*) Yes—yes, I'm waiting. (*She finishes the note—commences suddenly to speak into the telephone:*) Hello, Pimenov?—I'm at the hotel. I couldn't go on—I couldn't. . . . No, no don't—(*Long pause.*) . . . Just alone . . . Good night, good night, my dear—goodbye. . . . Pimenov, how is it going, badly? . . . Uh? . . . Whose dancing? . . . Desprez? . . . Oh—and how is it?. . . . Oh,—oh, I see—they didn't miss me? . . . They didn't miss me. (*She lets her hand drop with the receiver and goes on talking into the air.*) They didn't miss me—good night, Pimenov. . . . (*She is about to replace the receiver. She sits with it in her hand, unreplaced. The music has stopped. The room is strangely silent. Behind her the Baron peers from the closet. Her head sinks down upon her hands. A funny, singing noise comes from the telephone. She lifts the receiver to her ear. In a very strange voice, the voice of Ophelia, she speaks:*) Oh—I'm sorry, yes . . . I have finished. (*She replaces the receiver.*)

(The foregoing scene is much better played than described. It is, in fact, ballet.)

Quite calmly, Grusinskaya finishes the note on the table. She folds it up and places it in a prominent place on the table, or hangs it over the telephone. She crosses to the window, pulls back the curtains—the ones the Baron had been hiding behind a few minutes before.

We see the Baron watching. He glances at the door quickly. "No, there is not time." She is returning calmly. She crosses to the dressing table and takes the veronal out of a drawer. She looks at it thoughtfully, her lips are trembling a little. She moves to the radiator as if to seek warmth.

She sinks into a chair and her head droops over her folded hands which contain the veronal; she seems to pray.

The Baron comes from the closet—now is his chance, he looks at the door but can't make it. Looking on the floor for the key which Grusinskaya has previously thrown there, his eyes fall upon the note on the telephone—he reads it.

It is a farewell death note to Suzette—do not insert it. At this moment she has finished, the Baron returns to his hiding place. She makes the sign of a cross and goes to her bed.

She looks around nervously, apprehensively—like a deer who has heard something, then reassured, she places the veronal on the night table beside the glass of water. She is quiet and deliberate. She arranges the pillows under her head and lies down. She reaches for the bottle of veronal and empties it generously into her hand. She has to lean away upon one elbow, from the Baron's position, in order to balance herself.

The Baron steps like a cat from his hiding place. He goes to the bedside noiselessly and stands there.

She reaches for the glass—her hand stretches out for the glass. The Baron takes her wrist suddenly.

She turns quickly looking at him. The glass falls to the floor with a crash and breaks. As she moves, the veronal falls out of her hands upon the bed. She struggles up to a sitting position.

BARON

Please, do not be alarmed, Madam.

She glances up at him. She is bewildered. She seems to be coming out of a trance. Again she wants to jump from the window.

BARON

Careful—there's broken glass on the floor.

Now she becomes conscious of her near-nakedness. She draws her kimono tightly around her, glances across the wide expanse of bed. We see her consider passing over that way, but she is now a woman again—a woman of the earth—it would be a silly movement.

BARON

There.

He takes a pillow from the bed, throws it upon the floor over the glass, steps back. She gets up quickly and crosses, putting on her robe which was lying across the back of a chair.

Her first movement is not one of alarm but of—shame. She draws her robe more closely around her and looks at the Baron puzzled. She thinks, dreamily, "What is this?" She glances back at the veronal and the bed showing us plainly that she realizes this man must have watched her preparation for bed. We get a sense of relief with her. She is trembling.

The Baron has controlled his nerves perfectly. He senses his danger. He is caught red-handed with 500,000 marks worth of pearls in his pocket. He is wondering if she will ring the bell. For an instant he thinks of escape. He could dash for the balcony. He could strike her dead or silence her with threats. There is in the room an intoxicating sense of romance and danger. (It should be in the scene.)

BARON

Please do not be frightened, Madam.

GRUSINSKAYA

(*After a silence*) What do you want here?

BARON

Nothing—only to be here.

GRUSINSKAYA

Why do you hide in my room?

BARON

But surely you must know—because I love you.

GRUSINSKAYA

Because you love me—you love me?

She looks at him for a few moments and then suddenly she throws herself upon the bed and begins to weep more and more passionately.

BARON

(*Going over to her*) Poor little Grusinskaya!
Does it do you good to cry? Are you afraid?
Shall I go?

GRUSINSKAYA

I was so alone—always alone—and suddenly
you were there and said that. (*Sitting up*) No.
I am not afraid. It is strange.

BARON

Don't cry—it tears my heart to see you sob like
that.

GRUSINSKAYA

(*Regaining control*) Nerves—just nerves. You
must forgive me. I have had a bad evening. I am
very tired. Do you know what it is to be tired—
tired of a routine existence?

BARON

I'm afraid not—I usually do just what I feel like
doing at the moment.

*A look in his eyes reminds her of the strangeness of the situation. She rises
with returning dignity and pulls her robe around her—she is becoming
Grusinskaya of Imperial Russia; she is the woman grand dukes fought for.
She sweeps across the room.*

GRUSINSKAYA

So you felt like coming into a lady's room—and
you come. . . . What now?

BARON

(*Following her.*) I'd like to smoke a cigarette.

GRUSINSKAYA

Certainly.

*She grabs her cigarette box from the writing table and holds it out to him. He
takes a cigarete and lights it. She watches him curiously. She smiles, as she
watches him greedily inhale the smoke. She crosses and sits before her
looking glass. She brushes her hair back and powders her face. She looks
into the mirror, we feel that she has regained a desire to live. He crosses and
looks at her in the mirror. He smiles.*

GRUSINSKAYA

Why do you look at me like that?

BARON

I did not know you were so beautiful . . . and—

GRUSINSKAYA

(*Bitterly*) And then?—

BARON

No irony. You're so appealing—so soft—so
tired. I feel like taking you in my arms and not
letting anything more happen to you—ever.

GRUSINSKAYA

(*Involuntarily closing her eyes.*) And—and—

BARON

How tired you are!

GRUSINSKAYA

Yes—tired. . . .

BARON

So alone.

GRUSINSKAYA

Alone. All alone. (*Whispers in Russian.*) Oh,
you strange—strange creature.

BARON

You mustn't talk Russian to me.

GRUSINSKAYA

Strange man . . .

BARON

Am I quite strange to you?

GRUSINSKAYA

Not quite strange now. It is as if I had been
expecting you. You know, once when the Grand
Duke was alive, I found a man hiding in my
room—a young officer—

BARON

And? . . .

GRUSINSKAYA

He disappeared. Later he was found dead.

BARON

I never knew it was so dangerous to hide in a
woman's room when she's alone.
(*He embraces her.*)

GRUSINSKAYA

Go away. Who are you?—

BARON

A man who could love—that is all, who has
forgotten everything else for you.

GRUSINSKAYA

You could love me. It is so long since I have
heard that word. Nobody has loved me for a
long time. It is so icy-cold to be famous. One is
so cruelly alone. How is it that you—Let me
look at you. Your hands. Your eyes. Why could
you love me?

BARON

I saw you just now—then I saw you cry—and
now I see you in the mirror—Grusinskaya. . . .

GRUSINSKAYA

Grusinskaya. . . . Oh-oh if you knew how I
slaved and slaved for Grusinskaya—for the
success of Grusinskaya—for the triumph of
Grusinskaya . . . and what is she now? Just
someone who has found that on the day success
ceases, life ceases—Are you listening to me—
Do you understand?—I want you to understand.

BARON

Yes—I do understand.

GRUSINSKAYA

I think you must go now—the key is on the
floor.

BARON

I'm not going—You know I'm not going— Let
me stay here?

GRUSINSKAYA

I want to be alone.

BARON

That is not so—you don't want to be alone.

He looks back at the bed as if remembering the suicide attempt.

GRUSINSKAYA

I want to be alone—

BARON

No—You don't want to be alone at all—You
were in despair before—If I left you, you'd feel
worse than you did before. You must not be
alone—You mustn't cry—you must forget. . . .
Tell me that I can stay with you—tell me.

GRUSINSKAYA

(*Whispering*) Just for a minute then.

Outside the distant noise of Kringelein is heard—

BARON

What? Say it again—I didn't hear.

GRUSINSKAYA

(*She whispers.*) You—man. . . .

*The way she says it, the word goes home. It hurts him. She has looked into
his eyes for a moment with a strangely melting and almost happy expression.
She gets up suddenly. (Note: The other side of the bed—not where the glass
is.) She reaches with her feet for her slippers. She puts one on. She can't find
the other. Business as he gets other slipper for her. He kisses her ankle and
looks up at her. She smiles down.*

GRUSINSKAYA

Thank you—you are gallant. (*She turns, her
mood has changed.*) What a sentimental scene.
Grusinskaya weeping is a sight worth seeing. It
is many years since she did such a thing. . . .
You frightened me—badly. You're responsible
for this—painful scene.

*He watches her. The sound of her own voice reassures her. She is generating
warmth. Her cry has done her good, she speaks quickly, volubly.*

GRUSINSKAYA

The stage frays one's nerves. . . . the
discipline—it's so exacting. Discipline means
doing what you don't want to do and take no
pleasure in doing. Do you know what I mean?
Have you ever experienced the weariness that
comes from discipline?

BARON

I?—Oh, no. I do only what I take pleasure in
doing.

Grusinskaya turns; she is graceful again.

GRUSINSKAYA

I see—you do only what you take pleasure in
doing. You take pleasure in coming into a
woman's bedroom and you come. You take
pleasure in a dangerous climb onto a balcony, so
you do it. . . . And what is your pleasure now?

BARON

(*Naive as he says frankly.*) I should like to
smoke.

She rises. She had expected something else. His reply strikes her as chivalrous and considerate. She crosses to the writing table and brings back her little cigarette box which she holds out to him. He takes a cigarette and lights it. She watches him curiously. She smiles, as she watches him greedily inhale the smoke. She crosses and sits before her looking glass. She brushes her hair back and powders her face. She looks into the mirror; we feel that she has regained a desire to live. The Baron crosses and looks at her in the mirror; he smiles.

GRUSINSKAYA

Why do you smile?

BARON

Because I can see something in the mirror that you cannot. My dear—(*He pauses suddenly.*)

GRUSINSKAYA

What can you see?

BARON

You are beautiful!

GRUSINSKAYA

No.

BARON

Beautiful but so sad. I did not know it was so dangerous to look into a woman's bedroom.

Suddenly he stoops, takes her shoulder in his hands and kisses it. A long tender and sincere embrace. Her eyes close. A tremor passes through her. Suddenly his whole being is aware of her. She turns, rises and disengages herself.

GRUSINSKAYA

I think you had better go now. The key is on the floor.

He glances back. He speaks suddenly with an air of command.

BARON

I'm not going. . . . You know I'm not
going . . . Do you think I could leave you alone
here? After that?—

GRUSINSKAYA

What?

BARON

The veronal—you. I'm going to stay here with
you.

GRUSINSKAYA

I want to be alone.

BARON

That is not the truth. (*He catches her wrists.*)
You do not want to be alone—you're afraid of
being alone—I know you're afraid. I know you.
You were desperate, just now. If I go away
you'll be more desperate than ever. Say I am to
stay with you . . . say it. (*He almost shakes her.
Her head falls slowly on his chest.*)

GRUSINSKAYA

(*Whispers.*) For just a minute then. (*She pulls
away, crosses the room, quickly to the door, with
almost a cry. She looks around for the key to the
door.*) No—oh, no!

He crosses quickly to her and holds her in his arms.

BARON

Just for a minute, Grusinskaya—(*Outside the
distant noise of Kringelein and the Doctor.*) I've
never been so happy.

GRUSINSKAYA

What did you say?

BARON
I've never been so happy.

GRUSINSKAYA
Say it again—say it!

BARON
I have never been so happy!

KRINGELEIN and FLAEMMCHEN

Somewhere toward the end of the story, Lewis Stone as the hotel doctor says: "Grand Hotel. Always the same. People come and people go. Nothing ever happens." Well, this doctor must have been out on an office call during the twenty-four hours of the Baron's stay at the Grand Hotel. By the next morning, the Baron has managed to save Grusinskaya and give her a new purpose to her life; enchant Flaemmchen to a point where she has fallen in love with him—the poor, waif of a stenographer and the elegant aristocrat—a fantasy romance; and the Baron has raised mild Kringelein to the point where he considers himself something of a man in this world. However, also along the way, the Baron has managed to get himself shot and killed by Preysing, in Preysing's suite, with Flaemmchen as a witness to it; and Preysing, in good dramatic fashion, has gotten himself arrested and carted off to jail for the murder of the Baron. Of course, the hotel and management want to keep such unpleasant incidents "quiet."

KRINGELEIN'S ROOM

Kringelein opens the door and enters. Flaemmchen is looking into space. A lovely picture. Morning light over her hair, she is dressed.

KRINGELEIN
What's the matter?

FLAEMMCHEN
Oh—I was thinking—Poor Baron—Lying there,
his eyes so open.

KRINGELEIN

You loved the Baron, didn't you?

FLAEMMCHEN

Yes—

KRINGELEIN

So did I—He was friendly to me as no man ever was.

FLAEMMCHEN

Perhaps he really was a burglar—But they don't kill a man for that.

KRINGELEIN

He was in desperate straits. He'd been trying to raise money all day. He laughed—Poor devil! And then a man like Preysing kills him.

FLAEMMCHEN

(*Naively*) I didn't like Preysing right off.

KRINGELEIN

Then why did you have anything to do with him?

FLAEMMCHEN

(*Simply.*) Money!

KRINGELEIN

Yes, of course—money!

FLAEMMCHEN

You don't understand that do you?

KRINGELEIN

Of course I do—I never knew what money really
meant till I started spending it. Do you know—
(*He is silent for a moment.*) I can hardly believe
that anything so beautiful should come to me
from Preysing—I'll take care of you. Will—will
you let me?

FLAEMMCHEN

What?

KRINGELEIN

You'll have a good time with me. Want to? I've
got enough money. Ten thousand two hundred in
my pocketbook. Three thousand four hundred
that I won. It will last a long time. I can win
more—we'll travel.

FLAEMMCHEN

Yes—to Paris? I wanted to go there always.

KRINGELEIN

Wherever you like. Here I'll give you the money
I won, three thousand four hundred. Later you
can have more.

FLAEMMCHEN

Later?

KRINGELEIN

When I—I'm ill, Flaemmchen—It will not be
long—I'll not last long. Will you stay with me
until. . . .

FLAEMMCHEN

Nonsense! We'll find a great doctor, he'll cure
you. They can cure anything these days.

KRINGELEIN

Do you believe that you will have a better time
with me than you would with Preysing?

FLAEMMCHEN

Oh, yes, of course.

KRINGELEIN

(*Takes her hands*) Do you like me better?

FRAEMMCHEN

You're a good man, Mr. Kringelein—a very
good man.

*Kringelein straightens, happy, inspired, a smile on his face. He assumes this
posture. Takes the telephone.*

KRINGELEIN

(*Into telephone.*) When is the next train leaving
for Paris?— Yes. . . . Get two tickets for me . . .
and my bill please . . . and the lady's—Miss
Flaemm's . . . (*Puts down the telephone. To
Fraemmchen.*) We have to hurry. Let's pack—
we'll have breakfast on the train.

MUTINY ON THE BOUNTY

Incidents are made vivid in terms of the medium—the swish and
pistol crack of the lash, the sweating lean bodies, the terrible labor,
and the ominous judgment from the quarterdeck.

OTIS FERGUSON

M-G-M 1935
Produced by Irving Thalberg, Albert Lewin
Directed by Frank Lloyd
Screenplay by Jules Furthman, Talbot Jennings, and Carey Wilson
From the novel by Charles Nordoff and James Hall

AAN: Picture, Director, Actor (Charles Laughton, Clark Gable,
Franchot Tone), Screenplay, Musical Score, Editing

AA: Best Picture

CAST
Charles Laughton, Clark Gable, Franchot Tone, Movita, Dudley Digges,
Henry Stephenson, Donald Crisp, Eddie Quillan, Francis Lister,
Spring Byington, Ian Wolfe

Charles Laughton is unforgettable as Captain Bligh. The image of Bligh in the stern of his long boat, approaching the H.M.S. *Bounty* to take command of it, tells the audience all it needs to know about this man. You know this sailor, whoever he might be, is a tyrant—mean, petty, unscrupulous. He is the guy we're going to hate: the villain of piece. And it is screen acting at its best: the image tells all and prepares the audience for what is to come. For generations, Charles Laughton has been Captain Bligh and Clark Gable was Fletcher Christian without challenge to movie audiences. (Certainly not the unattractive remake in 1962 in which you sympathized more with the Captain Bligh of Trevor Howard due to the boorish and arrogant Fletcher Christian of Marlon Brando; or the 1985 version (which is supposedly based on the actual mutiny and not the novel about it) with Anthony Hopkins playing a Bligh that was merely stubborn and Mel Gibson as a Christian who was more of a dilettante, showing no real substance.)

The conflict between the tyrannical dictator and the humanistic rebel has been a story that has engaged audiences for many years, no matter where it is set, because it is a situation that can be translated in many guises into the audience's experiences, from the workplace to the conflicts between oppressive governments and its people. And in the 1930s fascist actions were much on people's minds.

That this film expresses its theme in a rip-snorting, fast-paced action adventure, told not in explosives and chases, but in human relationships and personal conflicts makes it all the better picture for it. It also relates its humanistic point of view to the audience without preaching.

A ship is a small, floating island-country surrounded by the sea. There is no democracy, no majority rule, no "let's take a vote" in a ship's company. The captain is the absolute authority and the court of only resort. And while the captain is absolute ruler, his first mate is his chief operating officer. If the captain and the first mate are in harmony as to the running of the ship, then all will be—we hope—smooth sailing. But when they are in opposition, then you can count on stormy seas ahead. The men aboard will side with one or the other, and the dissention will filter to the daily operation of the enterprise. And when one is fair and right, and the other is a petty tyrant and a crook— well, then, you have the makings for a possible classic.

The H.M.S. *Bounty* is on a two-year voyage before the mast on a scientific expedition to the South Seas. Since they have put out to sea there has been unrest in the way Captain Bligh has commanded the ship—not so much his ability as a sailor, which is above question, but as a commander and leader of men. He is paranoid and suspicious; he accuses his men of petty crimes without proof; he buys the worst supplies for his crew and pockets the difference for himself to feather his own nest. He severely punishes the men for the least offense—his punishments do not fit the crimes. Bligh rules by terror rather than govern by loyalty. Fletcher Christian, as first mate, has about reached the end of his tolerance of Bligh's tactics. His hostility toward his captain is about to surface.

CHRISTIAN and BLIGH

It was the practice of the British navy that the first mate should verify the "day books" (account records) of the captain of the ship as correct. It was also an open practice to pad such books. Bligh uses the custom to test the loyalty of Fletcher Christain.

INT. BLIGH'S CABIN ON THE BOUNTY—MORNING

We come in on Bligh in his cabin. He is finishing breakfast. The door opens and Christian enters.

CHRISTIAN
You sent for me, sir?

BLIGH
Good morning, Mr. Christian.

CHRISTIAN
Good morning, sir.

BLIGH
(*Affably.*) Had your breakfast?

CHRISTIAN
(*Dryly.*) Yes, sir—thank you.

BLIGH
(*More dryly.*) Hmmm—thought you might like
to join me—(*Begins to eat.*) Not bad, not bad,
the voyage so far—all hands accounted for—
only six down with scurvy—

CHRISTIAN
Five with scurvy, sir. One with flogging.

BLIGH
(*Gives Christian a sharp but humorous glance.*)
Correct, Mr. Christian. Does you credit. Five
with scurvy, one with flogging. (*Eating.*) But
we're still under canvas.

CHRISTIAN
(*Pointedly.*) Your seamanship, sir, is beyond
criticism.

BLIGH

(*Pleased, but modest.*) Thank you—all in the day's work. We should raise the Islands any day now—(*Very casually.*) Time we accounted for supplies—you'll find the ship's day-book—(*Points to ledger on table.*)—list of supplies issued on the outward voyage. (*Pause, eating.*) I'll be glad if you will certify—and sign.

CHRISTIAN

Certainly—(*He picks up the pen.*)

BLIGH

—matter of form.

CHRISTIAN

(*Looks up.*) This book is not correct, sir.

BLIGH

(*Looks up—winks broadly.*) Come, come—Mr. Christian—

CHRISTIAN

No such amounts have been issued.

BLIGH

Certainly not! (*Laughs heartily.*) Very smart, my lad—does you credit! You've signed day-books before, I'll warrant—with a few extra kegs in 'em that the ship never carried—

CHRISTIAN

I never bothered with accounts, as a rule, sir.

BLIGH

You will, when you're a captain. We all do it—(*Confidentially.*)—and we're fools if we don't. You know what a captain's pay is. Well, I'll stow away enough to keep me out of the gutter when I'm too old for service.

CHRISTIAN

(*Icily.*) I understand a captain's prerogative.
Ordinarily, I wouldn't give a hang—

BLIGH

(*Staring.*) Why is this case different?

CHRISTIAN

The captains I've served with before didn't
starve their men! They didn't save money by
buying up the stinking meat you put aboard at
Tenerife! They didn't buy yams that would
sicken a pig and force them on the crew!

BLIGH

Silence!

CHRISTIAN

They didn't call their men thieves, and
flog them to the bone when they complained
about it!

BLIGH

You impudent scoundrel! (*Raging.*) Sign the
book!

CHRISTIAN

I refuse. And you have no authority that can
make me!

BLIGH

I haven't—eh? I'll show you authority. Lay all
hands aft! *All hands aft!*

CHRISTIAN

(*Quietly.*) Very good, sir—

He turns and goes out.

BYAM

Byam (Tone) is a young midshipman whose first tour of duty was on board the *Bounty*. He took part in the mutiny because he, too, could no longer tolerate Bligh's fanatical treatment of the crew. But when it came to making the choice of running farther away or returning to England to face the music, Byam chose to the "noble" course. He, of course, was arrested and taken back to England in chains where he and a few other fellow mutineers were put on trial by the lords of the admiralty. The courtmartial has been concluded, and now the sentences (really foregone conclusions) are to be pronounced.

INT. NAVAL COURTROOM—DAY

Byam is brought in by a lieutenant with drawn sword and a guard of two marines, bayonets fixed. As he comes forward his eyes go to the table. Lying on the table before Lord Hood is a midshipman's dirk, the point toward Byam. Byam looks up slowly from the dirk, then steadily along the line of captains. He begins speaking in a low, firm voice, as CAMERA DRAWS BACK to include Bligh in a chair near the advocate.

BYAM

My Lord, much as I desire to live, I am not
afraid to die. Since I sailed on the *Bounty*, over
four years ago, I've known how men are made
qto suffer things worse than death—cruelly,
beyond duty, beyond necessity—(*Turns to
Bligh, his voice grows stronger.*)—Mr. Bligh,
you've told your story of mutiny on the
Bounty—how men plotted against you—seized
your ship—cast you adrift in an open boat—a
great venture in science brought to nothing—two
British ships lost—English seamen flung across
the world—drowned or killed by savages! But
there's another story, Mr. Bligh—(*Bitterly.*)—of
two cheeses and ten coconuts!—of a man who
robbed his seamen, cursed them, flogged them—
not to punish, but to break their spirit!—a story
of greed and tyranny, of anger against it—and
what it cost! (*Turns to Court.*) One man, my
lord, would not endure such tyranny!—(*Turns to
Bligh.*) That's why you hounded him, that's why

you hate him—hate his friends—that's why
you're beaten—(*Triumphantly.*) Fletcher
Christian is still free! (*Turns to Court, his tone
changing.*) But Christian lost too, my lord! We
all lost—on the *Bounty*! If Christian is alive he's
an outlaw hiding in despair from his own
countrymen! God knows he's judged himself—
more harshly than you can judge him! (*He turns
to spectators, looks off.*) I say to his father—He
was my friend—(*His voice breaks slightly.*)—A
finer man never lived! I do not justify his
crime—mutiny—(*Turns to Bligh.*) But I
condemn the tyranny that drove him to it! (*Turns
to the Court.*) You gentlemen know the uses of
authority—you exact the law of the sea. But the
letter of the law is one thing, the spirit is
another! I do not speak here for myself, not even
for the seamen you've condemned. I speak in
their names—in Fletcher Christian's name—for
all men at sea—Those men do not ask for
comfort, they do not ask for safety. If they could
speak, they would say, "Let us choose to do our
duty willingly, not the choice of the slave, but
the choice of free Englishmen." They only ask
the freedom that England expects from them.
(*He looks down at the table.*) Oh, if one man
among you believes that—one man!—he might
command the fleets of England, he might win
the seas for England—if he calls his men to their
duty, not by flaying their backs, but by lifting
their hearts! Their hearts, my lord to—
(*Overcome, he falters, almost breaks.*)—that
is all—

A long silence.

THE GREAT ZIEGFELD

Mammoth biopic which despite a few show-stopping numbers never takes off dramatically and becomes something of an endurance test; interesting, however, as a spectacular of it's time.

HALLIWELL FILM GUIDE

M-G-M 1936
Produced by Hunt Stromberg
Directed by Robert Z. Leonard
Screenplay by William Anthony McGuire

AAN: Picture, Actress (Luise Rainer), Director, Writing (original story), Interior Decoration, Editing, Dance Direction

AA: Picture, Actress, Dance Direction

CAST
William Powell, Luise Rainer, Myrna Loy, Frank Morgan, Reginald Owen, Nat Pendleton, Virginia Bruce, Ray Bolger, Harriett Hoctor, Ernest Cossart, Fanny Brice, Robert Greig, Jean Chatburn, Esther Muir,Gilda Gray, Leon Errol, Stanley Morner, Dennis Morgan

If you are planning to remake any of the films represented in this book and all you have is a hand-held video cam, stay away from this picture. There are few better examples of what is meant by the "classic Hollywood cinematic extravaganza" or the M-G-M studio style than this film, *The Great Ziegfeld*. One of the costumes used in the film required 2,000 yards of pleated chiffon. The musical number "A Pretty Girl Is Like a Melody" employed 182 male and female singers and dancers. The curtain for the set was 4,300 yards of rayon silk, weighing 1,800 pounds. It had 48 tripping lines, and the cyclorama for the number was 260 feet long, 80 feet high, and there were 6,000 flashing lights for the Milky Way. Over all, the script called for 105 speaking roles (not counting extras and "atmosphere"), and the final count was over 5,000 players used in the film. And the film had a playing time of three hours.

Florenz Ziegfeld, Jr. was one of the most successful producers in American theatre history, and perhaps its most famous. He had an unerring eye for glamour, taste, and talent, and today, over sixty years after his death, the term "Ziegfeld Girl" still epitomizes the best in female beauty. From 1907 to 1927, Ziegfeld produced an annual revue, "The Ziegfeld Follies," that not only redefined the revue, but also revolutionized it. He also was the producer of some of the most important landmark musicals of the 1920s, including the most significant of them all, *Showboat*. Ziegfeld was a first-rate showman, but he was also a serious theatrical producer.

The film centers on two events in Ziegfeld's life: his rise to fame and power as a producer, and the two marriages in his life—first to the musical comedy star Anna Held, and, second, the captivating actress Billie Burke. Interspersed between the marriages are musical interludes that represent, even more than Ziggy could do on stage, the opulence of his musical production numbers.

ANNA and ZIGGY

Ziggy (Powell) married his European star, Anna Held (Ranier), and she is devoted to him; but she is also moody and insecure in her career and in her marriage with him. She is a child in many ways, and Ziggy must be everything to her: husband, manager, father figure, and producer. Ziggy is an astute judge of her character and an expert in handling her moods.

INT. ANNA HELD'S SUITE—HOTEL SAVOY

Anna is in the suite, singing, with Pierre. Ziggy enters—but neither Anna nor Pierre notice his entrance. He sits down—his dog beside him. Then he sees the orchid on the floor, then another. He calls to Marie (the maid).

ZIGGY
Marie, somebody carelessly spilled the orchids.
Call Sidney for me and have him send another
dozen immediately.

Anna stops singing and glares at him.

ANNA
Why do you not pick these up?

ZIGGY
Because fallen flowers are like fallen stars—they
soon lose their luster.

ANNA

Marie—pick them up. (*Then to Pierre.*) Go
away, please—I cannot sing. I told you before I
am too angry to sing. Go—please! I am sick of
watching you roll your eyes like I do. (*Then to
Ziggy—who sits calmly as Pierre exits.*) So—I
am fallen star—yes? (*Ziggy smiles but does not
reply.*) I have no luster—no?

ZIGGY

Oh, yes—you have—but do you know what it is
from?

ANNA

I do not care!—What?

ZIGGY

Milk baths. At least, that's what you must tell
the reporters.

ANNA

Oh, I am so hurt—so humiliated! Ze front page
of ze paper say you are sued on my account. If
you must send me milk why do you not pay for
it?

ZIGGY

If I did, it wouldn't be in the papers.

ANNA

Couldn't you just tell them I used milk without
buying, and being sued for it?

ZIGGY

They wouldn't believe me. Now it's a matter of
court record—besides, they don't care whether I
ever pay the bill or not. All that interests them is
that in one month you've used twelve hundred
gallons of milk.

ANNA

Mon Dieu!

ZIGGY

(*To Marie.*) Marie, tell the reporters to come up.

ANNA

Marie—do nothing of the kind!

ZIGGY

You can't insult the press, Anna. (*He crosses to phone.*)

ANNA

(*As he takes the phone.*) If they come up I will tell ze truth!

ZIGGY

(*On phone.*) Desk, please. (*To Anna.*) At first don't tell them anything—pretend embarrassment.

ANNA

Pretend it? I was never so ashamed!

ZIGGY

Hello, desk clerk? Are the gentlemen of the press still waiting for Miss Held? If you will— thank you.

ANNA

(*Rushing to him.*) I will say I never take milk bath in my life—I will tell them it is a press story! I will go back to France. (*To Marie.*) Marie—pack ze zings! Quick! This time I mean it! (*Then to Ziggy.*) You cannot make ze circus of me—I am not ze strongman like Sandow—I do not lift horses. I am an artist. And never, never will I say this!

ZIGGY

(*On phone.*) Thank you so much. Ask them to
come up, please. (*To Anna.*) Don't you realize if
we put this story over, your name will be in
headlines from coast to coast and every woman
in America will be talking about you, and
imitating you?

ANNA

I do not care. I do not have to be cow to be a
success! (*Then going to desk.*) And before I
make such a fool of myself, I tear up my
contract with you. (*Then she excitedly looks for
the contract in the desk drawer, throwing other
papers aside.*) Besides, you do nothing as I like.
It must always be your way! I've asked many
times for costume like Lillian Russell's. She
does not have to take milk baths to be big
success. She is beautiful; but no—I cannot have
gown like hers! (*Then finding the contract, she
tears it up.*) There now—tell ze reporters about
that!

And Anna paces the floor again while Marie, singing gaily in French, can be
seen opening up the trunk again to pack.

ZIGGY

(*Softly, as Anna paces.*) Anna.

ANNA

I mean it—I am determined.

ZIGGY

(*In even softer tone.*) Anna.

ANNA

You tell ze reporters to come up—yes? Now I
will tell them everything!

ZIGGY

(*In even softer tone.*) Anna.

She continues to glare at him, but before his smile the anger suddenly leaves her face, and bursting into tears, she exclaims:

ANNA
Well—I should tell them—no?

ZIGGY
(*Tenderly.*) Anna.

And bursting into childlike tears, she drops her head on his shoulder, as he sweetly says:

ZIGGY
Now you do as I want you to, dear, and I'll do whatever you wish.

ANNA
(*Blubbering the words naively through her tears.*) You mean you'll let me have gown like Lillian Russell's?

ZIGGY
No, darling, you're not her type. But I'll tell you what I will do; I'll put ten Lillian Russells on the stage behind you.

She seems puzzled as she looks at him through her tears, but he gently places her head back on his shoulder; as the CAMERA MOVES from them to Marie, who, in disgust, is again unpacking the trunk.

ZIGGY and MARY LOU

Early in the film, Ziggy visits his father in his studio at the Chicago Conservatory of Music. Ziegfeld, Sr. is giving piano lessons to a little girl who has a crush on Ziggy. Years pass, and the little girl grows up. She comes to New York City, and she wants to see her beau from her childhood, who had promised then that he would marry her.

INT. ZIGGY'S OFFICE—DAY

The door is opened and Mary Lou (Chatburn) is shown in. Ziggy is at his desk, writing. He does not look up when she comes in. Mary Lou glances about the office. The walls are covered with pictures as was the hall, only these are more beautifully framed. Mary Lou looks at them fascinated—then to the grand piano on which she sees a picture of Anna Held—then on a wall over piano where there is a picture of Audrey Lane standing in the costume and on the steps of the "A Pretty Girl Is Like a Melody" number. Then seeing a big, high-backed chair facing his desk, Mary Lou sits down. Without looking up, Ziggy turns to his office phone and presses the buzzer.

> **ZIGGY**
> (*Into phone.*) Where's that girl you said was a friend of mine?

> **MARY LOU**
> Here I am.

Ziggy looks quickly—then as he puts up the receiver, she smiles and adds:

> **MARY LOU**
> I didn't want to disturb you.

Ziggy looks at her closely.

> **ZIGGY**
> Did you tell them outside you were a friend of mine?

> **MARY LOU**
> Yes, I did.

> **ZIGGY**
> I see—just to get into my office. Smart girl.

> **MARY LOU**
> I am a friend of yours. Have you forgotten me?

ZIGGY

(*Again looking closely, but trying to cover up.*)
No, of course not. I remember you very well.

MARY LOU

Who am I?

ZIGGY

(*Laughs, but is really trying to recall her.*) As if
I didn't know!

MARY LOU

Do you?

ZIGGY

Of course I do. I never forget the girl, the time,
or the place. (*Then leaning forward, he
murmurs.*) Atlantic City. (*Mary Lou shakes her
head in denial.*) It wasn't Atlantic City? (*Again
she nods her head negatively.*) That's strange. I
seem to remember a chair on the boardwalk with
you beside me, and. . . . Are you sure it wasn't
Atlantic City?

MARY LOU

It might have been Atlantic City—but it wasn't
me.

ZIGGY

Oh. . . . (*Then smiling suddenly.*) Now, I
remember. It was right here. You came to see
me about a year ago. Of course, it all comes
back to me. How are you, dear? Where have you
been? (*But Mary Lou is slowly shaking her head
negatively again.*) No?

MARY LOU

No. (*Then softly.*) You don't seem to remember
the girl, the time or the place. Perhaps this will
help you.

And she rises and crosses to the grand piano. She sits at the piano, then very simply plays the exercises we heard her play as a child. Ziggy watches her closely, then slowly realizes who she is. He sees her again as the kid in his father's studio. The vision passes. He leans forward across his desk, as he murmurs tenderly.

ZIGGY

Mary Lou! How is my girl?

Mary Lou stops playing and looks at him.

MARY LOU

(*As she crosses back to him.*) How is my fellow?

ZIGGY

(*Sitting and looking up at her as she stands before him.*)Well, well—my little Mary Lou is a big girl now, isn't she?

Suddenly Mary Lou throws her arms about him and kisses him fondly. He reacts to the kiss.

ZIGGY

Yes, indeed—she's a very big girl.

MARY LOU

(*As she sits on his lap as if it meant nothing.*) Are you glad to see me?

ZIGGY

Of course I am.

MARY LOU

Even if I wasn't at Atlantic City with you?

ZIGGY

Don't be silly, child—I knew it was you all the time.

MARY LOU

(*Waves Her finger at him doubtfully.*) Now— fibber!

ZIGGY

Of course I did. How long have you been in New York?

MARY LOU

One day.

ZIGGY

Have you seen my father lately?

MARY LOU

Yes—just before I left. And that reminds me— he told me to kiss you for him. (*And again she gives him a real kiss.*)

ZIGGY

(*As he gently pushes her away.*) Mary Lou, dear—I think in all fairness I should tell you— I'm a married man now.

MARY LOU

Yes, I know—I read about it. It broke my heart. (*She rests her head on his shoulder. He smiles, amused. Suddenly she straightens up and exclaims:*) But being married in New York doesn't mean anything, does it?

ZIGGY

(*Lifting her up off his lap.*) Oh, yes, it does, young lady. Come now—tell me why you're here and what I can do for you.

MARY LOU

First, I want to give you a big kiss for all the candy you've sent me.

ZIGGY

You've already done that twice. Now what?

MARY LOU

I want to go into the Follies. I've taken dancing for two years.

ZIGGY

How do your father and mother feel about it?

MARY LOU

I have no father or mother any more.

ZIGGY

I'm sorry, dear.

MARY LOU

Of course, Jimmy doesn't like it.

ZIGGY

Who's Jimmy?

MARY LOU

Oh, just another fellow I've been engaged to.

Ziggy laughs and presses buzzer.

ZIGGY

All right, Mary Lou—I guess I can take care of you.

MARY LOU

Can you take me to dinner tonight?

ZIGGY

No, I cannot. And if I put you in the show, I want you to promise to be a nice little girl always.

MARY LOU

I promise. May I say one thing before I go?

ZIGGY

Certainly. What is it?

MARY LOU

I forgive you for not marrying me.

And she exits.

FANNY, PRIMA DONNA, STAGE MANAGER and ZIGGY

One of the highlights of this film is that the real Fanny Brice appears as herself in a burlesque number, singing her signature song "My Man." In this scene Ziggy comes backstage of the burlesque house to offer her a spot in the next edition of the "Follies." (This film, and its "sequel," *Ziegfeld Follies* [1946]—in which Fanny Brice appears in a delightful sketch with Hume Cronyn—are two filmed records of just how special Fanny Brice was as a clown and comedic actress.) What is interesting about this particular scene is that it is a unique, independent unit in the screenplay. This scene is developed just as an actual revue sketch, complete unto itself, just as you might find in a stage revue of the period. This is one of the reasons it is included here.

INT. FANNIE BRICE'S DRESSING ROOM (DEWEY BURLESQUE)

It is a typical burlesque-house dressing room. There are two dressing table mirrors. Before one is the typical burlesque prima donna (Muir) trying out her voice a little, as she gazes at herself in the mirror. Fannie enters in costume of the "Fan Dance."

PRIMA DONNA

What's on now, Fannie?

FANNIE

(*Tired.*) Jimmy Barton.

PRIMA DONNA

He's not funny to me.

FANNIE

Don't be silly. That fellow is going to be a great
performer some day—he can make you laugh
and he can make you cry.

PRIMA DONNA

He makes me sick. Comedians bore me.

*Fannie shrugs her shoulders as if it were useless to argue and starts taking
off things, etc. Prima donna continues:*

PRIMA DONNA

And you give me a pain in the neck, too. Always
telling me who's going to be a great star. Once
in burlesque, always in burlesque—unless
you've got looks, or a voice, or something.

FANNIE

That's what I've got.

PRIMA DONNA

What?

FANNIE

(*Smiling.*) Something.

PRIMA DONNA

(*Patronizingly.*) Fannie, on the level—you don't
ever hope to get out of burlesque, do you?
You're good here because these people are from
Tenth Avenue. How good do you think you'd be
on Fifth Avenue?

FANNIE

Half as good.

*The prima donna gives her a look; and just then Fannie, who is pulling on a
stocking, exclaims:*

FANNIE

Darn it!

PRIMA DONNA

What's the matter?

FANNIE

Another silk stocking gone! Believe me, I'll
never buy a bargain from one of those stage-
door peddlers again!

PRIMA DONNA

You said that before. Why did you let the fellow
in?

FANNIE

He told the doorman he was Dillingham.

PRIMA DONNA

And you thought it was Mr. Dillingham, the
producer?

FANNIE

Naturally.

PRIMA DONNA

Calling personally to see you?

FANNIE

Well—I'll admit I was optimistic.

PRIMA DONNA

Oh, Fannie, why do you kid yourself?

FANNIE

Why do you discourage me? Suppose I am in
burlesque all my life—can't I dream a little in
the meantime? Can't I see myself in nicer
theaters, nicer clothes? After all, I'm the only
one looking.

And she pulls up a second stocking, only to have a run in it, too. She angrily pulls it off, as the stage manager comes to slightly open door.

STAGE MANAGER
Miss Brice, Mr. Florenz Ziegfeld is here to see you.

FANNIE
(*To prima donna*) Ah, ha! Another peddler!
First it's Dillingham, and now it's Ziegfeld!
(*Then to stage manager.*) Tell "Mr. Ziegfeld"
I'm not in, and if I was in, tell him I wouldn't
see him—and if I did see him, tell him I
wouldn't buy anything!

Just then Ziggy comes to the doorway, still carrying the mink coat over his arm.

ZIGGY
Pardon the intrusion, Miss Brice—I'm Mr.
Ziegfeld.

FANNIE
Is that so? (*To prima donna.*) Sarah, this is Mr.
Ziegfeld. (*Then to Ziggy.*) Mr. Ziegfeld, this is
Sarah Bernhardt.

ZIGGY
(*Kiddingly.*) Not the great Sarah Bernhardt!
Well, it certainly is a pleasure to run into you!

FANNIE
If you run into your friend "Dillingham," tell
him about the runs in his stockings.

ZIGGY
Do you know Charlie Dillingham?

FANNIE
Better than you know Ziegfeld. (*Then feeling
coat on his arm.*) Well, come on—how much do
you want for it?

ZIGGY

Miss Brice, I'm really here to offer you a great opportunity.

FANNIE

(*Still feeling the coat.*) I know—that's what they all say. What kind of fur is this?

ZIGGY

This coat? Oh, mink.

FANNIE

Is that so? And what is the price?

ZIGGY

(*Smiling.*) The original cost was twenty-seven hundred dollars.

FANNIE

Who cares about originals—copies are just as good! Can I try it on?

ZIGGY

Certainly. . . . (*As he helps her with coat.*) It should fit you very well.

FANNIE

Don't give me a sales talk—just tell me the price. I don't want to buy it—but I'll give you fifty dollars for it and not a cent more.

ZIGGY

It's yours, Miss Brice.

FANNIE

(*To prima donna.*) Stuck—again!

PRIMA DONNA

Are you really going to buy it, Fannie?

FANNIE

Say—if I can give Dillingham four dollars for silk stockings made of cotton, I can give Ziegfeld a little more for a mink coat made of skunk. (*Then to Ziggy.*) Besides, a bargain's a bargain. (*She takes money from a purse in the drawer of table, or from a trunk.*) Here's your forty dollars. Now get out before I change my mind.

Ziggy takes the money, bows to the ladies then suddenly bursts out laughing and exits. The prima donna starts feeling the coat as Fannie stands looking after Ziggy—frowning contemptuously at this "momser." Then suddenly the prima donna is all excitement. She exclaims:

PRIMA DONNA

Fannie!

FANNIE

What is it? Moths already?

PRIMA DONNA

Come here, quick! Feel—it's real mink!

FANNIE

How do you know? Did you ever have one?

PRIMA DONNA

No, but I've been promised one often enough to tell. It's real mink! It's probably stolen goods!

FANNIE

You mean it's hot?

PRIMA DONNA

Oh, of course it's warm—bet it's been smuggled in.

FANNIE

And I'll be arrested if I keep it?

PRIMA DONNA

Of course you will.

FANNIE

Call the manager! Call the police!

There is a knock on the door. Both jump nervously.

PRIMA DONNA

(*As Fannie puts coat behind her.*) Come in. . . .

The same stage manager opens the door.

STAGE MANAGER

Message for you, Miss Brice.

Fannie stands petrified as the prima donna takes the message and hands it to her.

FANNIE

You read it. I'm dying!

The prima donna opens the envelope and forty dollars drops out. Fannie stares incredulously as the prima donna reads:

PRIMA DONNA

"Dear Fannie Brice: I can't accept your forty dollars, but you can please me by accepting the coat. I shall expect you at my office in the New Amsterdam tomorrow, as I want to engage you for the Follies. Florenz Ziegfeld, Jr." (*To Fannie.*) Fannie, it was him—it was Ziegfeld! How do you like that!

FANNIE

(*With faraway look.*) I like it. (*And she swoons— and collapses to the floor—as prima donna bends over her excitedly.*)

PRIMA DONNA

Fannie, Fannie—speak to me. Have you fainted?

FANNIE

Can't you see I have, you chump! Get me some
whiskey!

ZIGGY and BILLIE

Ziggy has been divorced by Anna Held, and is gaining a reputation (deserved
or not) on the Great White Way as a lady's man. Attending a society dance,
Ziggy becomes fascinated with one of the most bewitching actresses reigning
on Broadway at the time, Billie Burke (Loy). Billie, as was the custom of the
time, was under *exclusive* contract to a rival producer. Under the terms of
such a contract, a star was not allowed much public exposure. The theory
behind this ploy was that the more a star was kept out of the public eye, the
more mystery she exuded from the stage. Producers were, quite frankly, dic-
tators concerning the private lives of their actors in such situations.

Billie has been allowed an outing by her producer, as long as she stays in
the presence of her escort, Jack Billings, one of the producer's major associ-
ates. (Billings is a friend of Ziggy and has a running rivalry with him
throughout the film's story.) This, of course, makes no difference to Ziggy;
in fact, this makes it a bit more fun and a challenge.

INT. A BALLROOM. NIGHT.

*The Paul Jones is being danced. Men and women circle the room, each
taking the other's hand as they do so. CAMERA CRANES in close as Ziggy
comes to Billie Burke. The whistle blows as he dances with her.*

ZIGGY

(*As they dance.*) Do you mind if I tell you I don't
like your name, Miss Burke?

BILLIE

You don't? Well, there's a way you can change
it—if I happen to like yours.

*The whistle blows again, and again the men and women circle the floor—and
again when Ziggy comes to Billie Burke the whistle blows.*

BILLIE

(*As Ziggy again gets to her.*) Hmmmm—we
meet again.

Ziggy smiles. Billie looks up at him, already strangely fascinated.

BILLIE

(*As they dance.*) Well—aren't you going to tell
me?

ZIGGY

Tell you what?

BILLIE

Your name.

ZIGGY

It really isn't important. Ask Mr. Billings.

BILLIE

I will if I can ever get to him again—but you
seem to stand in with the whistle.

ZIGGY

I do. When I was a little boy I loved to whistle—
and a whistle never forgets.

*Again the whistle blows—and again they circle the room—still again, when
Ziggy and Billie touch hands, the whistle blows.*

BILLIE

(*As he takes her again.*) Oh, this is really too
much! Aren't you getting bored?

ZIGGY

Are you?

BILLIE

I'm afraid not.

ZIGGY

Tired?

BILLIE

Are you?

ZIGGY

I'm afraid so—I'd much rather just talk. (*He stops at a door leading to the balcony, opening it.*) Do you mind?

With a happy laugh, Billie walks out onto the balcony. He follows her. In the distance are the electric signs of Broadway. One prominently has the name of Ziegfeld on it.

ZIGGY

(*Looking beyond.*) Don't you love the lights of New York? To me they're more beautiful than all the landscapes in the world.

BILLIE

More beautiful than the mountains of the West?

ZIGGY

I think so. (*Then.*) Is it too cold for you?

BILLIE

No, indeed—I'm enjoying it. The electric signs fascinate me. (*Then she murmurs, as she reads signs.*) Wrigley's Chewing Gum—Fleishman's Yeast—Ziegfeld's—

ZIGGY

(*Very casually.*) Do you know Ziegfeld?

BILLIE

I don't want to—I understand he's a horrible person.

ZIGGY

Horrible?

BILLIE

Yes. They say he's a terrible ladies' man. I
suppose that's forgivable, though—he's
surrounded with so many girls.

ZIGGY

Strange you never met him.

BILLIE

I don't want to. I love his shows—they're
always so beautiful and in such good taste! It
would disappoint me terribly to meet him and
discover him a fat, pudgy man with a big
stomach.

ZIGGY

But he really isn't fat; and I don't think he's so
pudgy.

BILLIE

Do you know him?

ZIGGY

Very well. He'd like you.

BILLIE

How do you know?

ZIGGY

Didn't you say he had good taste?

BILLIE

(*Laughs.*) You're sort of a ladies' man yourself,
aren't you?

ZIGGY

With you as the lady, I could make Ziegfeld look like an amateur.

BILLIE

(*Laughing.*) But you haven't told me your name yet.

Just then Billings enters from the ballroom.

BILLINGS

(*As formal as Will Hay's collar.*) If you don't mind, Mr. Ziegfeld—Miss Burke, with the special permission of her producer, Mr. Frohman, came to this affair with me tonight. And if you have no objections, I would like one dance with the lady! (*He offers Billie his arm.*)

BILLIE

(*Staring at Ziggy.*) Mr. Ziegfeld! . . . (*Then smiling, she adds:*) Well, you were right—he isn't pudgy. (*Then to Billings, as she rests her hand on his arm.*) Shall we go in?

ZIGGY

Don't I get another dance?

BILLIE

I'm afraid not.

ZIGGY

Perhaps I could see you home?

Billings frowns.

BILLIE

(*Smiling.*) I'm afraid not.

ZIGGY

I imagine it's Mr. Frohman you're really
afraid of.

BILLIE

Perhaps.

ZIGGY

He doesn't want you to be seen too much
socially—is that it?

BILLIE

Frankly, no, he doesn't.

ZIGGY

And you're going to be a good little girl and
obey.

BILLIE

Frankly, yes, I am.

ZIGGY

And besides, you don't like me very much
anyway.

BILLIE

Frankly, I don't.

*Billings bursts out laughing and leads her into the ballroom. CAMERA
HOLDS on Ziggy. He looks after them—an expression in his eyes that we
have never seen before. He has fallen in love with this fascinating creature.
There is a tenderness in his expression, a certain reverence curiously
congruous with the wholesome beauty of the girl herself.*

ANNA and MARIE

Luise Rainer won the first of her two Oscars in this film as Anna Held, and this is the scene that captured the gold for her.

Anna has read in the paper of the marriage of Ziggy and Billie Burke. Anna is still—as always—very much in love with Ziggy, even though she is the one who divorced him. She has also been ill. She is even now more melancholy because of the news. But she is going to put on a brave face, be the good ex-wife, and call her former husband to offer him her congratulations. By the time Luise Rainer as Anna got off the phone there wasn't a dry eye in the movie house, and the Academy was engraving the statuette with her name on it.

INT. ANNA HELD'S HOTEL SUITE—DAY

Anna Held holds a newspaper with headlines announcing Ziggy and Billie Burke have married. Anna is in a simple negligee. She is resting on a chaise lounge in her hotel suite. Marie is with her. She is putting some medicine in a glass partly filled with milk and stirs it as she watches Anna let the paper fall to the floor. Then as Anna rises she offers her the glass.

> ANNA
>
> No thanks, Marie—I'm tired.

> MARIE
>
> It's your medicine, Madame.

> ANNA
>
> I know—but I'm tired of it.

She crosses to the piano on which is set a picture of Ziggy in a silver frame.

> MARIE
>
> (*Solicitously—watching her intently.*) Perhaps now Madame would like to go to Paris for a while?

> ANNA
>
> No, Marie—I'm too tired to go anywhere—or do—anything.

Marie picks up the paper and quietly folds it and is stealing away with it, when Anna, without looking away from the picture, speaks:

ANNA

Marie, look in the paper, please, and tell me—
where did they go on their honeymoon?

MARIE

Oh, they could not go anywhere, Madame. Miss
Burke is appearing in the play here. We saw her
only two weeks ago. Remember—you insisted,
Madame?

ANNA

Oh, oui—I know. We enjoyed her so much, too.
She is a lovely actress, Marie.

MARIE

Oui.

ANNA

She has such twinkling eyes—and such a
nervous little twitter when she speaks. (*Her eyes
turn to picture again as she continues:*) I can
imagine Flo being in love with her.

*Tears start to come to her eyes. CANERA PANS as she goes to the window—
the tall window of the old Savoy Hotel—and looks out. She doesn't want
Marie to see her tears—but Marie is watching her, her own eyes a little
moist.*

ANNA

(*Without turning, and putting a sort of false
courage into her voice.*) Marie, call his office. I
will—congratulate him.

*Marie picks up the phone, and while watching Anna, doubtfully calls the
number.*

ANNA

(*As if reassuring herself.*) I should wish him
luck—oui?

MARIE

Oui, Madame. (*Then into phone.*) Hello. Mr.
Ziegfeld, please. Anna Held calling . . . oui.

ANNA

(*Suddenly unable to go through with the plan,
breaks out.*) No, no, Marie! Hang up! I cannot
talk to him now—I. . . .

MARIE

Hello, Mr. Ziegfeld. (*Then hopelessly holding
the phone out she adds in a whisper to Anna:*)
He's on the telephone, Madame.

*Anna pulls herself together and bravely crosses to the phone. She seats
herself at the table, and as she takes the phone she forces herself to smile.
Then, in a cheerful voice, even though her cheeks are wet from the tears she
has just shed:*

ANNA

Hello, Flo. This is Anna. I am so happy for you
today, I could not help calling to congratulate
you. Oh, wonderful, Flo! Never better in my
whole life! I'm so excited about all my new
plans . . . oui. I'm going to Paris for a few
weeks, then I'm coming back to do a new show
and . . . Oh, oui—it's all wonderful. I'm so
happy about it—and I—I hope you are happy,
too. Oh, that is nice. I'm so glad for you. (*Then,
though brokenhearted, she laughs through the
following words:*) It sounds very funny from ex-
husband and ex-wife to be telling each other
how happy they are—oui? Yes, Flo. Thank you.
Goodbye . . . (*Then as she replaces receiver.*) . .
. darling.

*All through the above, as she forces cheerfulness into her voice, a smile to
her face, Marie, behind her, weeps for this brave little woman. As she hangs
up, Anna's head drops to the table and she sobs out:*

ANNA

Oh, Marie!

And the weeping Marie cries out:

MARIE

If you loved him so much—why did you ever
divorce him?

ANNA

(*Her head still on the table.*) Because I thought it
would bring him back to me, Marie! I was sure it
would bring him back to me.

ZIGGY and BILLIE

Nothing in show business is forever, and Ziggy has had a run of bad luck
with shows—compounded by his extravagant expenditures and lifestyle. He
has also had a conversation in a barbershop with three strangers who have
pronounced him as "washed up." Aside from that aspect of the story, this
sequence of scenes contrasts the differences in Ziggy's marriages and his
relationships with his two wives. With one he had to be the master; with
Billie he has a supporter and helpmate as well as severest critic and staunch
friend.

INT. LIVING ROOM OF ZIEGFELD HOME—DAY

*Billie is again glancing at the script, but as Ziggy stands at a mirror fixing
his tie, she steals a glance at him. She has detected a worry he has tried to
hide. In the mirror Ziggy catches her glance, her puzzled expression.*

ZIGGY

What's the matter, Billie?

BILLIE

Nothing, dear. Why?

ZIGGY

I thought you seemed sort of worried. It really
wasn't very expensive.

> **BILLIE**
>
> I don't mind—she loves it. And it does look cute
> on her little wrist.

Ziggy turns from mirror, his tie set.

> **ZIGGY**
>
> Do I look better?

> **BILLIE**
>
> Much.

> **ZIGGY**
>
> What are you reading?

> **BILLIE**
>
> A new play. Charming part, Flo—I think I'll
> do it.

> **ZIGGY**
>
> You mean go back on the stage?

> **BILLIE**
>
> Why not? Patricia's not a baby anymore.
> Besides the salary might help to make up some
> of the losses of your new show.

> **ZIGGY**
>
> I don't need your help, Billie—I don't need
> anybody's help. I'm quite all right—and I don't
> want you to go back on the stage.

ZIGGY'S BEDROOM. UPSTAIRS.

*Billie enters and pauses thoughtfully before the door. Then she opens it
quietly and enters. CAMERA moving with her. Ziggy sits on foot of bed, his
head buried in his hands. Billie goes to him, gently touches back of his bowed
head, and without looking up, he puts his arms around her waist.*

BILLIE

What's wrong, Flo.

ZIGGY

I'm all through, Billie.

BILLIE

(*Smiling.*) Through with what, dear?

ZIGGY

Everything. I'm slipping. I'm all washed up. I'm getting old.

BILLIE

And who told you all that?

ZIGGY

(*Still with head bowed.*) Three men in a barber shop.

BILLIE

So that's why you forgot your tie.

ZIGGY

Yes. (*Then looking up pathetically.*) And I've never done anything like that before in my life!

BILLIE

Isn't that tragic? For the first time in your long career, you forgot a tie. (*She laughs and sits beside him.*) Who were these men, Flo?

ZIGGY

I don't know. I never saw them before, but they said I'd never do another hit.

BILLIE

And what did you say?

ZIGGY

I told them—I'd have four on Broadway at one time!

BILLIE

That sounds more like you.

ZIGGY

Yes—but it was only a bluff. (*Then kissing her hand.*) I'm sorry, Billie. I didn't mean to worry you. (*He rises and takes her hands.*) Shall we go to dinner?

But Billie doesn't rise. She sits looking up at him.

BILLIE

Flo, I'm disappointed in you. I didn't think you'd ever lose confidence in yourself. It's been your sublime superiority more than anything else that has made up for so many of your faults— and you have faults, dear, you know that. (*Then suddenly.*) I don't mean that I'm jealous of you. I'm not, because with your love of beauty, you can never be cheap or common. So, in whatever you do—you need never fear me—but what is much more important, don't be afraid of yourself. (*She rises, kisses him gently, then crosses to picture on wall, pushes it aside, exposing a safe. She opens it, then turns to him.*) In here is all the jewelry you've ever given me— even the queen's crown. Thousand of dollars worth; and many more thousands in bonds I bought myself before even meeting you. I've been saving it all for Patricia—but I'm going to give it to you—on one condition. (*Ziggy stares at her—he can't speak. She goes on:*) And that is—you keep your promise and have four hits on Broadway!

THE LIFE OF EMILE ZOLA

Rich, dignified, honest and strong, it is at once the
finest historical film ever made and the greatest screen biography.

NEW YORK TIMES

WARNER BROTHERS 1937
Produced by Henry Blanke
Directed by William Dieterle
Screenplay by Heinz Herald, Geza Herczeg, and Norman Reilly Raine
From a story by Heinz Herald and Geza Herczeg

AAN: Picture, Director, Actor (Paul Muni),
Supporting Actor (Joseph Schildkraut), Writing (original story, screenplay),
Interior Decoration, Music Score, Sound, Assistant Director

AA: Picture, Supporting Actor, Writing (screenplay)

CAST
Paul Muni, Joseph Schildkraut, Gale Sondergaard, Gloria Holden, Donald
Crisp, Erin O'Brien-Moore, John Litel, Henry O'Neill, Morris Carnovsky,
Ralph Morgan, Louis Calhern, Robert Barrat, Vladmir Sokoloff,
Harry Davenport, Robert Warwick, Walter Kingsford

This film does not cover the entire life of Emile Zola, and that is one of the
reasons it works. The film concentrates most of its energies and time on
the most dramatic conflict in Zola's life, his defense and efforts to exonerate
Captain Alfred Dreyfus, who had been sentenced to Devil's Island for life for
treason, and the consequences such a fight had on Zola and his life.

Zola became convinced that Dreyfus was the victim of a criminal conspiracy perpetrated by French army commanders who manufactured evidence
to bolster their weak case. They conspired to cover up their own mistakes
and to protect their own reputations—and the truth be damned: what is the
life of one innocent man compared to the reputation and honor of the French
army? Dreyfus was a perfect fall-guy for the army because he was mild-
mannered, Jewish, and from the German speaking province of Alsace. (The
Dreyfus affair still haunts the French military and the French government
today, nearly a century after Dreyfus's conviction and ninety years after his
exoneration and reintegration into the French army. The ramifications of the
affair still engender impassioned debates between contemporary Dreyfusards
and anti-Dreyfusards.)

As portrayed in the movie, Zola (Muni) is a writer who is fanatical in his pursuit and recording of the truth. Along with the rest of France, Zola assumed that Dreyfus (Shildkraut) was guilty because those in positions of trust and power said so and presented proof of their convictions. Then new material is brought to his attention by the wife of the unfortunate Captain Dreyfus. To facilitate the re-opening of the case, Zola wrote and published one of the most famous newspaper essays in history, *"J'accuse"*(I accuse), opening himself up to libel. Zola put himself at great personal risk and at both financial and professional ruin to prove the innocence of man who was a total stranger to him—and for the pursuit and revelation of the truth.

ZOLA and MME. DREYFUS

Zola has reached the pinnacle of his profession: he is one of the most popular and respected writers in France; he has a comfortable home and income; and he has just received notification that he's been elected to the prestigous French Academy, the ultimate recognization of his work. His friend, the painter Cezanne (Sokoloff), thinks Zola has become soft and complacent— the fire that made him unique has gone out. To this troubled Zola comes one of the last persons he wants to meet, Madam Dreyfus (Sondergaard), who has been badgering anyone of importance about her husband's innocence and begging him to examine the evidence she has amassed proving Dreyfus was framed.

MED. SHOT—INT. ZOLA'S LIVING ROOM—NIGHT

It adjoins his study. Lucie Dreyfus is standing near the fire, nervous and distraught. She is holding a portfolio of documents. Melting frost glitters on the fur of her coat. On the mantel is the self-portrait of Cezanne. As Zola enters, Mme. Dreyfus looks quickly up. Zola crosses and bows, prepared to dismiss her; but something in her lovely, tragic face prevents him.

ZOLA
Madame Dreyfus ? . . .

MME. DREYFUS
Yes, Monsieur Zola. (*Hurriedly.*) Please forgive
me for intruding like this but (*Desperately.*)—I
had to see you—talk to you about my husband.

ZOLA

(*On his guard.*) But, Madame, what can I do for
your husband?

MME. DREYFUS

(*Blurting it out.*) He is innocent, Monsieur
Zola— (*Holding up the portfolio.*) I have
absolute proof—but no one will listen. No one—
(*Her voice drifts off.*)

ZOLA

(*Gently.*) Naturally, as his wife, you believe him
innocent. But, Madame, he was lawfully
convicted.

MME. DREYFUS

(*Flaring—bitterly.*) Lawfully convicted—for a
crime he did not commit! . . . (*Then pleading
frantically:*) Please, Monsieur—you are the only
man in all France that can make them listen—
All your life you have stood for truth and
justice—

She is trembling as she stops and gazes at him with haunted, imploring eyes.

ZOLA

(*Troubled by her gaze—beings to pace.*) But,
Madame—I'm hardly the one to help you— I'm
just an ordinary citizen—I have my work—my
books to write—!

MME. DREYFUS

(*She looks up quickly, a ray of hope in her eyes.*)
A certain Colonel Picquart—

ZOLA

Oh—that! It was all in the papers. Picquart came
back from Africa and accused Esterhazy of
writing the bordereau, but Esterhazy was
acquitted, Madame!

MME. DREYFUS

(*Bitterly.*) Of course he was! Acquitted by the same army group that convicted my husband!— Even though Esterhazy's own banker testified that it was Esterhazy's writing on the bordereau—not my husband's!

ZOLA

(*Trying to break her down.*) But three hand-writing experts testified that the writing was your husband's!

MME. DREYFUS

(*Scornfully.*) Hand-writing experts?—tools of the General Staff! (*Then frantically.*) Don't you see?— They had to acquit Esterhazy, to save the face of the General Staff! They'll stop at nothing to protect themselves! They are even ready to sacrifice one of their own class!—

ZOLA

(*A little annoyed.*) Ah, that is fantastic! —Childish! The General Staff has more important work to do than—(*Turning to her abruptly*) What do you mean—sacrificing one of their own class?

MME. DREYFUS

(*With quiet deliberateness.*) Colonel Picquart was arrested and imprisoned in Mount Valerien early this evening!

ZOLA

(*Incredulously.*) They've arrested Picquart?— Why?—What has he done?

MME. DREYFUS

(*With a bitter smile.*) Nothing—nothing except speak the truth!

ZOLA
(*Impatiently.*) We must deal in facts, Madame—
not irony.

MME. DREYFUS
(*Eyeing him intently.*) I have all the facts,
Monsieur Zola—here—

*She quickly opens the portfolio and takes out a number of letters which she
hands to Zola as she continues with tense eagerness.*

MME. DREYFUS
These are copies of letters written to Colonel
Picquart by the Assistant Chief of Staff, proving
beyond doubt that the General Staff knows
that my husband is innocent and Esterhazy is
guilty! . . .

ZOLA
(*Looks up from the letters a little agitated.*)
Why weren't these used in the Esterhazy court-
martial?

MME. DREYFUS
(*With quiet irony.*) Colonel Picquart is a good
soldier—He kept silent at the command of his
superiors.

ZOLA
(*Outraged.*) They knew—and they ordered him
to suppress the truth? Why, that's monstrous!

CUT TO:

WIDER ANGLE

*He crosses to the mantlepiece. Madame Dreyfus, feeling that she has
succeeded in interesting him, pleads passionately:*

MME. DREYFUS
Monsieur Zola—you will help me, won't you?

Zola makes no reply, but commences to pace up and down. He taps his fist irritably with the letters, an angry, agitated little bourgeois whose comfort and security are threatened. Zola suddenly turns to face her. . . .

ZOLA

How can anyone help you? All France believes
your husband guilty—hates him as a traitor—
Don't you see?—They would hurl down and
destroy any man who would dare champion him!

MME. DREYFUS

(*Desperately.*) But surely there must be some
way to right this terrible wrong!—

ZOLA

(*Shaking his head.*) Your husband's case is
officially closed. (*Beginning to pace again*)
There's nothing can be done . . . (*Then as if
thinking outloud.*) . . . unless some fool would
publicly accuse the General Staff—and get
himself dragged into court on a charge of
criminal libel—Then possibly—

He stops suddenly, afraid that he has said too much. He turns to see Madame Dreyfus' imploring look. Sensing her plea, he crosses to her quickly, as he tries a little desperately to justify himself.

ZOLA

You wouldn't honestly expect—Why—a man
has his family to consider—his
responsibilities—himself! I've lived my life—
I've had enough of fighting and turmoil—
(*Gesturing around the room.*)—I've worked
hard to achieve all this . . . you can't ask me to
throw it away—I am happy—contented here—
you must leave me to enjoy it—(*He stops
suddenly a little shamefaced that he has let his
real reason slip out. He turns away from her.*)

The painful silence is broken by Madame Dreyfus' tired voice, as she sees her last hope collapse:

MME. DREYFUS

I am sorry, Monsieur Zola. . . . It was only my
despair that brought me here. I was thinking of
my husband—condemned to suffer a living
death—(*Then trying to control her emotions.*)
I had dared to hope—that perhaps—if you
would—(*Choking up, she rises quickly.*)
Goodnight, monsieur!—(*She hurries out of
the room.*)

*Zola looks after her compassionately a moment; then, seeing the letters in his
hand, he calls after her as he crosses toward the door:*

ZOLA

Madame Dreyfus—just a moment! You've—

*He stops as he hears the sound of the closing door OVER SCENE. He is
troubled as he looks at the letters in his hand; then he crosses back slowly to
the chair in which Madame Dreyfus sat. He sees the portfolio she has left
behind. He picks it up; he is tempted to examine its contents, but then his
face hardens as he throws it back on the chair. As he starts to pace the room
again with nervous and uncertain agitation—*

CUT TO:

*Zola looks at the Academy letter. Then Zola looks at the picture of Cezanne.
He tears up the Academy letter and starts writing.*

ZOLA

Zola examined the materials Mme. Dreyfus left behind the night she visited
him. He has become convinced on his own that Dreyfus is innocent and the
victim of a conspiracy by the highest ranking military and government officials. Zola's righteous indignation energizes him into action. His action is to
write "*J'accuse—*." He takes it to the offices of the newspaper *L'Aurore* to
read it to, among others, Labori, an attorney, and Clemenceau. Zola intends
to expose a scandal that will rock France and the careers and personal lives of
both prominent government and military officials and private citizens and to
correct a most grievous wrong and concealment of the truth.

NEWSPAPER OFFICE—DAY

Zola unwraps his manuscript, and smiles grimly at Labori . . .

ZOLA

Labori, you're going to be a busy man!
(*Quiet tenseness.*) Clemenceau—I'm going to
explode a bomb—I call it—"A Letter to the
President of the Republic." (*Zola fingers his
manuscript in silence, then he commences to
read.*) "Mr. President of the Republic . . . Permit
me to tell you that your record, without blame so
far, is threatened with a most shameful blot—
this abominable Dreyfus affair! A court-martial
has recently, *by order*, dared to acquit one
Esterhazy—a supreme slap at all truth—all
justice! But since they have dared, I too shall
dare! I shall tell the truth—because if I did not,
my nights would be haunted by the spectre of an
innocent being expiating under the most frightful
torture a crime he never committed. (*Zola
pauses to remove his pince-nez and wipe his
eyes. The room is still and tense; Clemenceau
sits on the edge of his seat, hands gripping the
chair arms. Zola resumes, speaking with
increasing fire and conviction.*) It is impossible
for honest people to read the iniquitous bill of
accusation against Dreyfus without being
overcome with indignation and crying out their
revulsion! (*Ringing tones.*) Dreyfus knows
several languages—crime! He works hard—
crime! No compromising papers are found in his
apartment—crime! He goes occasionally to the
country of his origin—crime! He endeavors to
learn everything—crime! He is not easily
worried—crime!

CUT TO:

MED. CLOSE SHOT—ZOLA READING

ZOLA

He *is* easily worried—also a crime! (*Turns a page.*) The Minister of War, the Chief of the General Staff, and the Assistant Chief *never doubted* that the famous bordereau was written by Esterhazy. But the condemnation of Esterhazy involved revision of the Dreyfus verdict—and *that*, the General Staff wished to avoid at all cost! For over a year, the Minister of War and the General Staff have known that Dreyfus is innocent, but they have kept this knowledge to themselves. *And those men sleep, and they have wives and children they love*! (*Pause.*) Dreyfus cannot be vindicated without condemning the whole General Staff! That is why the General Staff has screened Esterhazy *. . . to demolish Dreyfus once more*! Such then, Mr. President, is the simple truth! It is a fearful truth!—But I affirm with intense conviction— The truth is on the march, and nothing will stop her! (*Zola pauses again, to polish his glasses. A deathly stillness prevails in the room, so much so that when Clemenceau knocks a small object from the desk to the floor the others start. Zola resumes reading:*) Mr. President, it is time to conclude. (*Pause, then in ringing tones.*) *I accuse* Colonel Dort of having been the diabolical agent of the affair, and of continuing to defend his deadly work through three years of revolting machinations! *I accuse* the Minister of War of having concealed decisive proofs of the innocence of Dreyfus! *I accuse* the Chief of Staff and the Assistant Chief of Staff of being accomplices in the same crime! *I accuse* the Commander of the Paris Garrison of the most monstrous partiality! *I accuse* the handwriting experts—Messieurs Belhome, Varinard, and Couart of having made lying and fraudulent reports! *I accuse* the War Office of having vilely led a campaign to misdirect public opinion and cover up its sins! *I accuse*—

CUT TO:

MED. CLOSE SHOT—ZOLA

ZOLA

—the first court-martial of violating all human
rights in condemning a prisoner on testimony
kept secret from him . . . and *I accuse* the
Esterhazy court-martial of having covered up
this illegality *by order*, thus committing in turn
the judicial crime of acquitting a guilty man! (*As
he speaks—*

CAMERA DRAWS BACK

Zola's listeners are enthralled.

ZOLA

In making these accusations I am aware that I
render myself open to prosecution for libel. But
that does not matter! The action I take is
designed only to hasten the explosion of truth
and justice! Let there be a trial in the full light of
day! (*Zola's hand holding the paper, drops—his
head goes up*) I am waiting! . . .

ZOLA

Zola has gotten his wish: He's been brought to trial for criminal libel against
the military establishment and certain specific officers. However, his defense
has been thwarted by the machinations of army officals and the Minister of
War. Zola and his attorneys are not allowed to enter or even address certain
facts about the case because the Ministry and commandants have consistently
said that it is "sensitive" or classified material that would go against "national
security" if introduced or testified about. As a final stand, Zola asks to be allowed to address the jury in his own defense.

   (It must be remembered in considering the trial of Zola that in the French
Napoleonic Code of Justice a defendant is automatically considered by the
state as *guilty* and has *to prove himself innocent*; while in the
Anglo/American justice system the burden of absolute proof of guilt is on the

prosecution's shoulders. It is a major difference in the approach to justice between the French and the Anglo/American judicial systems.)

THE COURTROOM—DAY

Zola walks to the witness stand. He waits there, polishing his glasses and looking myopically around, a poor, great man, buffeted by this adventure in the autumn of his life. He is not a heroic figure. He seems used and wearied by his ordeal. There is something of the "poor lawyer" about him. Yet he is calm, and when he speaks it is with a note of unconquerable pride.

CUT TO:

MED. CLOSE SHOT—ZOLA

He replaces his glasses, peers around, then begins to speak to the jury. His voice at first low, dispassionate.

ZOLA
Gentlemen . . . in the House of Deputies, a month ago, to frantic applause, the Prime Minister, Monsieur Meline, declared that he had confidence in you twelve citizens, into whose hands he had bestowed the defense of the Army. In other words, you were being instructed *by order*, to condemn *me*, just as, in that other case the Minister of War dictated the acquittal of Esterhazy!

PRESIDENT OF THE COURT
(*Thunderous interruption.*) The Prime Minister gave no such order to this jury!

CUT TO:

ZOLA
(*Firing up.*) His words made his intention to coerce justice unmistakable! And I denounce them to the consciences of honest men! (*Again quietly.*) However, my profession is writing— not talking. But from my struggling youth until

today, my principal aim has been to strive for truth. That is why I entered this fight! All my friends have told me that it was insane for a single person to oppose the immense machinery of the law . . .

                                        CUT TO:

MED. CLOSE SHOT—GROUP OF GENERALS AND OTHER OFFICERS

as they listen intently.

ZOLA'S VOICE
. . . the glory of the army, and the power of the state. (*After a pause.*) They warned me that my actions would be mercilessly crushed . . . that I would be destroyed! But what does it matter if an individual is shattered, if only justice is resurrected?

                                        CUT TO:

CLOSE SHOT—ZOLA

ZOLA
It has been said that the state summoned me to this court. That is not true. I am here because *I* wished it! *I alone have chosen you as my judges! I alone* decided that this abominable affair should see the light so that France might at last know all and voice her opinion! My act has no other object—my person is of no account. I am satisfied! (*Leaning earnestly forward.*) But my confidence in you was not shared by the state. They did not dare say all about the whole, undividable affair, and submit it to your verdict. That is no fault of mine. You saw for yourselves how my defense was incessantly silenced. (*With emotion.*) Gentlemen—I know you!

                                        CUT TO:

FULL SHOT—THE JURY

leaning intently forward.

ZOLA'S VOICE
You are the heart, and the intellect, of my
beloved Paris where I was born, and which I
have studied for forty years. I see you with your
families under the evening lamp. . . .

CUT TO:

CLOSE SHOT—GROUP OF WORKMEN AMONG SPECTATORS

ZOLA'S VOICE
I accompany you into your factories—your
shops. You are all workers—and righteous men!

CUT TO:

CLOSE SHOT—RAT IN OBSCURE CORNER OF COURTROOM

struggling and scrabbling at wall in effort to get free.

ZOLA'S VOICE
You will *not* say, like many: "What does it
matter if an innocent man is undergoing torture
on Devil's Island? Is the suffering of one
obscure person worth the disturbance of a great
country?

CUT TO:

MED. CLOSE SHOT—ZOLA

ZOLA
Perhaps, though, you have been told that by
punishing me you will stop a campaign that is
injurious to France. Gentlemen, if that *is* your
idea, you are mistaken! Look at me! . . .

CEMERA MOVES UP TO: CLOSE SHOT—ZOLA

ZOLA
Have I the look of a hireling—a liar—a traitor? I
am only a free writer who has given his life to
work, and who will resume it tomorrow. *And I
am not here defending myself.* (*Pauses.*)
Tremendous pressure has been put upon
you."Save the army! Convict Zola and save
France!" I say to you (*Ringing tones.*)—*Pick up
the challenge!* Save the army! And save France!
But do it by letting truth conquer!

CUT TO:

TWO SHOT—MME. LUCIE DREYFUS AND MATHIEU DREYFUS

He is tense. Her hands are tightly clasped. Both faces are wet with tears.

ZOLA'S VOICE
Not only is an innocent man crying out for
justice; but more—much more—a great nation is
in desperate danger of forfeiting her honor! So
do not take upon yourselves a fault, the burden
of which you will forever bear in history.

CUT TO:

CLOSE SHOT—ZOLA FROM ANOTHER ANGLE

ZOLA
A judicial blunder has been committed. The
condemnation of an innocent man induced the
acquittal of a guilty man . . . and now today you
are asked to condemn me because I rebelled on
seeing our country embarked on this terrible
course. (*Terrific, impassioned plea.*) At this
solemn moment, in the presence of this tribunal
which is the representative of human justice,
before you, gentlemen of the jury, before France,
before the whole world—

I swear that Dreyfus is innocent! By my forty
years of work, by all that I have won, by all that
I have written to spread the spirit of France, I
swear that Dreyfus is innocent! May all that melt
away—may my name perish— if Dreyfus be not
innocent! *He is innocent!*

*He stands, silent for a moment; then, as he steps down a storm of protest,
shrieks, yells of "Liar! Liar!" . . . "Down with him!" . . . "Throw him in
the Seine!" stamping and whistling turn the courtroom into a bedlam.
The President demands order and gets it.*

ALEXANDRINE and ZOLA

Even though Zola was found guilty of libel and had to flee into exile to
England to escape going to jail, eventually the truth was exposed, just as Zola
believed all the time: That nothing can stop truth once it's on the march.
Dreyfus has been exonerated, and Zola has been able to return to France, this
time with honor.

But Dreyfus's case has also done something else for Zola. It has
rekindled his creative juices, and Zola is now obsessed with finishing what he
thinks will be his most important work. He works at a punishing pace
because he fears he will not live to finish it—this his most important work.
His wife of many years, Alexandrine (Holden), is more concerned about
Emile her husband than she is about Zola the writer finishing his greatest
achievement.

MED. SHOT—ZOLA'S WORKROOM—
RUE DE BRUXELLES—NIGHT—SEPTEMBER, 1902

*The room is furnished luxuriously, as before, and a bright fire is burning on
the grate. A clock on the mantel points to a quarter to twelve. Zola is working
furiously at his desk. His hair is in disarray and he works with a strange,
possessed energy. Suddenly he stops writing and looks through his books on
the desk as if for a reference. Not finding it, he gets up and crosses to the
bookshelves. He finds a book and starts leafing through it.*

CUT TO:

MED. CLOSE SHOT—ZOLA—SHOOTING TOWARD THE DOOR TO WORKROOM

Alexandrine, a robe over her nightdress, comes through the door, and seeing Zola absorbed in his book, calls to him:

ALEXANDRINE
Please, dear. . . . It's past midnight. You've done enough tonight.

Zola darts her a glance as he gives an impatient little snort. . . .

ZOLA
Enough?

He puts down the book. It is not what he wants. He mounts the ladder to the upper shelves.

ALEXANDRINE
(*A little sharply.*) Emile—you must come to bed.

Zola, balanced on the ladder, peers myopically along an upper shelf of books.

ZOLA
(*Without looking at her.*) Presently, my dear— presently. (*Suddenly breaking off irritably.*) Confound the maid and her dusting! (*Then to Alexandrine.*) Alexandrine, what's become of my military dictionary? You know—the big green one?—

Alexandrine sees the book lying on the desk before her. She replies to him a little nonplussed. . . .

ALEXANDRINE
Why, Emile, isn't this it? (*She holds out the book to him.*)

ZOLA
(*Grinning a little sheepishly.*) So it is.

(He quickly comes down from the ladder and crosses to the desk. He opens the book and starts leafing through it in search of some reference. Alexandrine watches him a moment, quizzically.

ALEXANDRINE

Must you drive yourself like this day and night?

Zola, his nose in the book replies quickly with strange insistence . . .

ZOLA

I must, Alexandrine, I must—there's so much to do—and so little time to do it. . . . (*Then straightening and looking before him.*) I see it all clearly now—the cause and the effect—the roots and the tree—(*He stops, struck by the phrase.*)

ALEXANDRINE

But, darling—

ZOLA

(*Gesturing her to silence.*) Wait a minute— (*Then repeating the phrase critically.*)"The cause and the effect—the roots and the tree . . . " (*With sudden conviction.*) I can use that! (*He bends over the desk and starts to jot it down.*) Now what were you saying, my dear?

ALEXANDRINE

(*Trying to be patient.*) I said—I can't understand all this frantic hurry. There's always tomorrow—

ZOLA

(*Looking up quickly.*) Always?— I wonder?— (*Then slowly, as if with premonition.*) I wonder—if, in the middle of my most important work, there will always be a tomorrow? . . .

ALEXANDRINE

(*A little concerned.*) Please—you're tired—

Zola, not listening, continues as if reasoning to himself.

ZOLA

What matters the individual—if the idea
survives?

ALEXANDRINE

(*A little more firmly, as she tries to break his
mood.*) Now, Emile—you must get some rest.
You've got to be up early for the Dreyfus
ceremony.

ZOLA

(*Slowly coming out of it.*) Yes—Dreyfus—
Tomorrow he will be restored to the Army.
(*Then suddenly turning on Alexandrine with an
ironic smile.*) You know, it's a queer thing—this
whole Dreyfus business— (*Starting to pace the
room.*) Before it—I thought my work was
done—I could sit back—dream a little. . . .
(*Pointing up at the Cezanne portrait.*) Cezanne
was right—I was getting smug and
complacent—then suddenly—poof! (*Gesturing
an upheaval.*) —came the Dreyfus explosion—
and I'm alive again—my head bursting with
ideas!—

*Then suddenly pointing to the manuscript on his desk, he continues with
mounting excitement and fervor. . . .*

ZOLA

That new book—it's bigger than anything I
dared before. . . . (*Crossing to her at desk.*)
. . . The world about to hurl itself to
destruction—the will of nations for peace—a
powerful brake—stopping it on the brink!—

Alexandrine, overwhelmed by his bubbling energy, stares at him.

ZOLA

(*Thinking her incredulous.*) You don't believe
it?—Wait!—

Finding a page in his manuscript on the desk, he begins reading from it:

ZOLA

"To save Dreyfus, we had to challenge the might
of those who dominate the world. It is not the
swaggering militarists! They are but puppets that
dance as the strings are pulled— it is those
others—those who would ruthlessly plunge us
into the bloody abyss of war, to protect their
power and their gold! . . . (*Looking up from
paper.*) Think of it, Alexandrine!—(*With
mounting indignation.*) Thousands of children,
sleeping peacefully tonight under the roofs of
Paris—London—Berlin—all the world—

CUT TO:

CLOSE SHOT—ALEXANDRINE

She reacts with horror as his voice continues OVER the SCENE.

ZOLA

—doomed to die horribly on some titanic
battlefield—unless it can be prevented.

CUT TO:

MED. CLOSE SHOT—THE TWO

ZOLA

(*Continuing with fierce determination.*)—And it
can be prevented! (*Pacing as the thoughts pour
out of him.*) The world must be conquered—not
by the force of arms, but by ideas—ideas that
liberate! Then can we build anew—build for the
humble—and the wretched. . . .

*He stops suddenly, his head cocked to one side, critically. Then he nods as he
comments to himself with frankness.*

ZOLA

That's good—I mustn't forget that. (*He hurries to his desk, sits, and starts writing it down, mumbling as he writes.*) "The world—must be conquered—force of arms—"

CUT TO:

CLOSE SHOT—ALEXANDRINE

She is staring at him, a little troubled by his strange elation, as his voice continues to mumble OVER the SCENE:

ZOLA

"—but by ideas—that liberate—"

CUT TO:

MED. CLOSE SHOT—THE TWO

She bends over and kisses him tenderly on the hair.

ALEXANDRINE

Goodnight—Emile.

ZOLA

(*Pecking brusquely at her hand.*) Goodnight, my dear—goodnight. (*Continuing to write and mumble.*) "Then we can build anew—"

Alexandrine gives him a last quizzical look, and starts out of scene. Zola continues to write, completely absorbed.

ZOLA

"—build—for the humble—and the wretched—"

As the pen scratches in silence—

DISSOLVE TO:

INT. ZOLA'S WORKROOM—LATER THAT NIGHT—CLOSE-UP—THE CEZANNE PORTRAIT

—hanging over the mantle of the fireplace. The boring eyes of Cezanne are looking off in silence that is broken only by the ticking of the mantle clock.

The CAMERA PANS DOWN to the Clock—and we see that it is now a quarter past three in the morning.

The CAMERA PANS DOWN further to the fireplace. The coal fire in the grate is burning badly. Little tongues of yellow flame leap fitfully from the half-burned coal. Thin wisps of smoke spiral upwards, only to be forced down by the improper draft of the chimney. OVER the SCENE comes the intermittent sound of coughing, as the CAMERA PULLS BACK—MOVING ALONG THE FLOOR as if in the path of the coal gas, till it stops on a:

CLOSE SHOT—ZOLA—AT HIS DESK

He is still writing furiously. His hair is disarranged, his collar open. He pauses, raises his head, and passes his hand over his brow as though dizzy. There is perspiration on his face. He coughs once or twice; then engrossed in his writing, returns to it. He completes the page, reaches for another, and continues to write

CUT TO:

CLOSE SHOT—FIREPLACE

The wisps of smoke curl downward from the throat of the fireplace.

CUT TO:

CLOSE SHOT—ZOLA. IN WORKROOM

His violent coughing makes him stop writing again. Then, shaking his head to clear it, he forces himself to write again. As he starts—

CUT TO:

CLOSE SHOT—PAPER ON ZOLA'S DESK

(Half a sentence he has already written reads:)
"One dare not remain passive in such a grave
hour, when the iniquitous forces of the past—"
*(Zola's hand comes into scene and completes the
sentence, writing with increasing effort, as his
voice continues its coughing—)*"—offer
supreme combat to the energies of tomorrow—"
*(The hand pauses, the fingers tighten their grip
on the pen and write again with distinct effort:)*
    "I hope I shall not die before I see the rising of
a new—" *(The hand falters. The fingers relax
their grip. The pen falls from the hand which
gradually goes limp.)*

ANATOLE FRANCE

Zola died from carbon monoxide poisoning caused by noxious gasses coming
from coal heating while woprking at his desk in his poorly ventilated study.
There was inadequate ventilation in the workroom due to Zola's obsessive
fear of drafts and his concern that they would bring him ill-health. (In the
film, one of the early "plants" about Zola's character was his fear of drafts
and his continually closing windows and other ventilations. This device was
used to prepare the audience for the accidental death two hours later .)

    Zola's memorial service is held at the Pantheon, one of the historic
buildings in Paris. His eulogy is delivered by another of France's great writers, Anatole France (Carnovsky), destined himself to be a Nobel Prize
Laureate.

FULL SHOT—INT. PANTHEON—PARIS—DAY

*Filled with the brilliant uniforms of the high officers of the army and the
diplomatic corps, and the formal dress of statesmen and the prominent
people of France. Hundreds of ordinary Parisians are also present.
Charpentier, Labori, and other friends of Zola in foreground Nearby, in full
uniform, is Major Dreyfus with Madame Dreyfus and Mathieu Dreyfus.*

*Zola's coffin is standing on a pedestal. Chiseled in the stone of the pedestal
are the words: EMILE ZOLA. Nearby Anatole France stands alone.*

OVER the SHOT, SOUND TRACK carries the music of the "Eroica" played softly by an invisible orchestra.
CAMERA MOVES UP TO:

MED. CLOSE SHOT—ANATOLE FRANCE—DAY

standing at the tomb of Zola and facing dignitaries.

ANATOLE FRANCE
Let us not mourn him, let us rather salute that bright spirit of his which will live forever; and, like a torch enlightened a younger generation inspired to follow him. Take to your hearts the words of Zola enjoying today's freedom; do not forget those who fought the battles for you, and brought your liberty with their genius and their blood. Do not forget them; do not applaud the lies of fanatical intolerance. Be human—for no man in all the breadth of our land more fervently loved humanity than Zola. He had the simplicity of a great soul. He was enjoying the fruits of his labor—fame, wealth, security—when suddenly he tore himself from all the peaceful pleasures of his life, from the work he loved so much— because he knew that there is no serenity, save in justice . . . no repose, save in truth!

CUT TO:

MED. CLOSE SHOT—ALFRED, LUCIE, AND MATHIEU DREYFUS

With the Dreyfus children beside them, they listen intently. The children are ten years older than when Dreyfus was rehabilitated.

ANATOLE FRANCE
In those dark days of his sacrifice and suffering, many a good citizen saw the moral downfall of France! Justice, truth, honor—all seemed lost!

CUT TO:

CLOSE SHOT—ANATOLE FRANCE

His voice rises—trumpets out.

ANATOLE FRANCE
Yet all was saved! (*Increased emphasis.*) Zola
not merely laid bare a miscarriage of justice!
(*Powerfully.*) At the sound of his brave words
France awakened from her sleep!

*Through the balance of this scene, as Anatole France continues, CAMERA
DRAWS BACK so we see, in succession, Anatole France speaking, the
Madame France and Zola's tomb, the close mourners, such as Alexandrine
and Zola's friends, etc., the brilliant figures of army, diplomacy and state,
then gradually the multitude and the whole interior of the Pantheon, giving
an impressive general view of the grandeur and magnitude of the ceremony.
But the voice of Anatole France does not lose volume.*

ANATOLE FRANCE
(*With great emotion.*) The consequences of his
actions unfold themselves today in might and
majesty! He inspired great social and judicial
reforms whose forward march sweeps all before
it. Gentlemen, how admirable is the genius of
our country, how beautiful the soul of France,
which for centuries taught right and justice to
Europe and the world! France is once again the
land of reason and benevolence because one of
her sons, through an immense work and a great
action gave rise to a new order of things, based
upon justice, and the rights common to all men!
(*Pause.*) Let us not pity him because he suffered
and endured! Let us envy him! (*Solemn and
spiritual.*) Let us envy him, because his great
heart won him the proudest of destinies. . . .
(*Like a trumpet call.*) *He was a moment of the
conscience of Man!*

*As Anatole France's last words ring out and die away, the music of the
"Eroica" swells and grows to infinite grandeur as we—FADE OUT*

MRS. MINIVER

That almost impossible feat, a war picture that photographs the inner meaning, instead of the outward realism of World War II.

TIME MAGAZINE

M-G-M 1942
Produced by Sidney Franklin
Directed by William Wyler
Screenplay by George Froeschel, James Hilton,
Claudine West, and Arthur Wimperis
From the novel by Jan Struther

AAN: Picture, Actor (Walter Pidgeon), Actress (Greer Garson), Supporting Actor (Henry Travers), Supporting Actress (Dame May Whitty, Teresa Wright), Director, Screenplay, Cinematography (b&w), Sound, Editing

AA: Picture, Director, Actress, Supporting Actress (Teresa Wright), Screenplay, Cinematography

CAST
Greer Garson, Walter Pidgeon, Teresa Wright, Richard Ney, Dame May Whitty, Peter Lawford, Henry Travers, Reginald Owen, Henry Wilcoxon, Helmut Dantine, Rhys Williams, Aubrey Mather

The first image the film gives of Mrs. Miniver (Garson) is that of a woman rushing down a crowded city street in a stylish, flopping sun hat. She has something terribly important and bothersome on her mind. So bothersome, in fact, it makes her get off her bus and miss her train home. It turns out, however, that the bothersome problem is whether to buy a new hat or not—a temptation she gives into.

This moment of characterization is a brilliant illustration of where Mrs. Miniver starts in her world, a middle-class housewife whose life is on an even keel and whose worst problem is how to tell her husband she's bought a new hat. The journey Mrs. Miniver takes through the film, with her life, home, family, and country turned upside down by the upheaval of war and the very real threat of invasion, turns her into a woman of resilience, fortitude, resourcefulness, and unexpected depths of bravery she didn't know she had. Mrs. Miniver is the personification of a whole island nation that fought on alone during the dark, early days of World War II, against frightful odds, to keep the black monster of Nazism at bay. It's no wonder this film grasped the heart strings of the American nation and that of the Academy. It handily won the Best Picture of its year. As Winston Churchill suppposedly wrote to Louis B. Mayer, the film *Mrs. Miniver* is "propoganda worth a hundred battleships."

Mrs. Miniver follows the lives of an ordinary, middle-class English family affected by the events of World War II, yet who also try to carry on with a normal day-to-day life as much as possible, under extremely trying circumstances, including falling in love, marrying, attending flower shows, and losing loved ones to the fates of war. It is through the Minivers' determination to remain as "normal" as possible that we see their resilience, fortitude, and stubbornness—against the odds—develop and mature.

MRS. MINIVER and GERMAN PILOT

England is at war with Nazi Germany. The Blitz is in full swing. Among local happenings, a German pilot (Dantine) has been downed and is on the loose somewhere in the vicinity. Mrs. Miniver is up early because she has not been sleeping well. Her son is one of the young pilots trying to ward off the Nazi invasion, and her husband, Clem (Pidgeon), was called out of bed five days before to take the family boat to an unrevealed spot. Clem is participating in Churchill's audacious and desperate plan to evacuate the British army from Dunkirk before it can be destroyed by the advancing Nazi hordes; the plan is to use every private and commercial boat in the U.K. over thirty feet in length. As both wife and mother, Mrs. Miniver has a lot more to worry about than whether or not to buy a new hat.

It is early in the morning. Mrs. Miniver is up, anxious, concerned for the return of both her husband and her son. It is a beautiful morning, sun shining, and since her garden extends to the riverbank, Mrs. Miniver wanders down to the boat's mooring dock, hoping that just looking into the distance will bring her husband safely home.

(N.B.: In the film, the part of the milkman, kept here, was reduced to a non-speaking, background figure kept outside the kitchen.)

EXT. MINIVERS' GARDEN AND NEARBY RIVERBANK—DAY

Mrs. Miniver stands a moment, listening to the sound of the guns. Then she moves down to the river's edge, from where, unobstructed by trees, she can see down the stretch of water. There is no boat in sight, no sound save the fading rumble of the guns. She sighs—starts up to the garden again.

Suddenly she stops, stares off, puzzled and alarmed. She expresses fear and moves closer to CAMERA; staring off.

SHOT FROM HER ANGLE

Protruding from a clump of shrubs near the hedge are the feet and legs of a man in German aviator's uniform. The boots are muddy and worn.

MRS. MINIVER AND GERMAN AIRMAN

Mrs. Miniver, frightened, hesitates a moment, then takes another step forward that brings the body of the enemy pilot into view. His face is hidden in his arms as he sleeps the sleep of utter exhaustion; his slim form suggests youth. His uniform is stained and bedraggled. Mrs. Miniver stares, fascinated a moment. Then, rather losing her head, she turns swiftly and runs up the noisy gravel path toward the house. CAMERA PANS with her rapid flight. Suddenly a voice snaps out like a pistol shot.

> **GERMAN**
> Stehen bleiben! Oder ich schiess! (Stand still! Or
> I will shoot!)

She stops dead, terrified. The German comes into scene, gun in left hand. She slowly turns to face him.

> **GERMAN**
> Move or make noise—I shoot!

Mrs. Miniver is too frightened to speak. She makes a sign of assent with her head.

> **GERMAN**
> Alone?

> **MRS. MINIVER**
> My children are upstairs—And the maid—all
> fast asleep.

> **GERMAN**
> Food—drink.

MRS. MINIVER

All right.

She turns toward the house. The German springs forward to intercept her. (By now it becomes clear that his right arm is hanging almost helpless at his side. But in spite of his youth, his wound, the weakness of hunger and exhaustion, the German maintains an attitude of cold control and ruthless determination. We feel he is too self-possessed to shoot Mrs. Miniver without cause but also that he would do so without a moment's hesitation if she gave him the slightest uneasiness. For her part, Mrs. Miniver, when over her first fright, seeks to detain him in the hope that something may happen that will lead to his arrest.

GERMAN

No! I come!— No noise!

Mrs. Miniver leads the way into the house. The German follows closely, gun in hand. As they go:

DISSOLVE TO:

KITCHEN AT "STARLINGS."

as Mrs. Miniver and the German enter. He menaces her with the gun and speaks in a sharp whisper.

GERMAN

Food! Quick—

MRS. MINIVER

I'm getting it—but don't wave that gun at me—
you're frightening me—

She is getting out some bread. Before she can hand it to him, he snatches it and stows it away in his pocket. Using his right hand, he winces with pain and fumbles badly at his pocket.

GERMAN

Milk—hurry!

She takes a milk bottle from the icebox. He grabs it, again registering the pain in his right arm when he tries to lift it high enough to tilt the bottle into his mouth. He swallows greedily, still watching her, so that little runnels of milk dribble down the front of his uniform. He drops the empty bottle on the table and asks in an urgent whisper:

GERMAN

You have meat?

MRS. MINIVER

Yes, I think I—

She searches the icebox.

GERMAN

Hurry!—

MRS. MINIVER

I'm being as quick as I can!—

She brings out a piece of ham. The German snatches it and is about to tear off a piece with his teeth when we suddenly hear footsteps outside the house, the rattle of milk bottles and the cheerful whistle of a popular tune. Footsteps approach. The German instantly shoves the bit of ham inside his shirt, flattens himself against the wall near the door and keeps the door covered with the gun. The whistling man is seen passing an open window—

MRS. MINIVER

(*Whispering.*) It's the milkman—he won't
come in.

The German never takes his eyes off the door, through the glass panel of which we now get the silhouette of the milkman's head as he stoops to put the bottle on the step. Still whistling the milkman starts away. Mrs. Miniver stands tense, as though hesitating whether to cry out or not. The milkman crosses by the open window again, catches sight of Mrs. Miniver, stops. We see the German crouched agains the wall quite near him, but just out of sight.

MILKMAN

Mornin', Ma'am—you're up early—

CLOSE SHOT—MRS. MINIVER

She hesitates—glances toward:

CLOSE SHOT—THE GERMAN

His gun is on the door, but his eyes are on her, warning her.

CLOSE SHOT—MRS. MINIVER

MRS. MINIVER

(*To milkman.*) Yes—yes, I am—

MILKMAN

Well, it's a lovely mornin'—

We hear him start away, whistling again. The whistling grows more distant.

KITCHEN—LONGER SHOT

As the whistling recedes the German starts to edge toward the door.

MRS. MINIVER

I wouldn't go yet—he serves the next house, too.

The German signals to her impatiently to shut up. He is listening intently. The whistling dies away. The strain is relaxed, the gun wavers, it is clear that the German is on the verge of collapse. He touches his damaged arm with the hand that holds the gun.

MRS. MINIVER

You're wounded.

He ignores her speech. He has food and drink, he now wants a coat to cover his uniform.

GERMAN

(*Urgently and imperiously.*) Coat!

She hesitates a second, then turns and moves toward door to dining room.

GERMAN

Wait!—I come!—

He follows her to the dining-room door. Over his shoulder as he stands at the open door, his gun on her, we see her cross the dining room and go through open door to hall. She is always in sight as she opens a closet, takes out a coat and returns with it. The German backs into the kitchen before her, indicates with a gesture that she shall put the coat on a chair a couple of feet from him. She does so. He gestures sharply that she shall withdraw. She moves back.

CLOSE-UP—MRS. MINIVER

She stands looking off at the German. She has more or less recovered her nerve. There is a flash of calculation in her eyes. This man is a menace. He should be trapped. But how?

SHOT OF THE TWO

The German, failing to put on the coat with his wounded arm, puts the revolver into his right hand and tries to get into the coat with the aid of his sound left arm. Mrs. Miniver stands watching him. An exclamation of agony is forced from him by some movement. He bends over the chair, clutching it with one hand for support.

MRS. MINIVER

That arm! It's hurting you!

She takes a step forward.

GERMAN

(*Bowed, pain-racked, savage.*) Stand away!

She stops, frightened. He stands bent over for a moment. She ventures:

MRS. MINIVER

You should have help. Won't you let me call a
doctor?

GERMAN

(*Fiercely.*) NO! (*He slowly straightens himself,
his eyes dazed with pain.*) You—help—

He slumps into a chair, still holding on to the revolver.

MRS. MINIVER

I'll do what I can— (*She comes to him, looks at
his arm.*) Why it's stiff with blood! We shall
have to slit that sleeve . . . Just a moment—

*She goes to the sink, fills a bowl with hot water, brings the bowl to the table,
takes scissors from the table drawer and sets to work to slit the sleeve. He
reacts to the agony of having his arm touched, but faces it grimly and never
releases the gun from his left hand. When the arm is bared, Mrs. Miniver
gives a little cry of horror.*

MRS. MINIVER

Oh! . . . It must have been septic for days! You
can't go on with an arm like that! You're only fit
for a hospital—

GERMAN

Hurry!—

MRS. MINIVER

Very well—but you're being very foolish. I'll
try to clean that wound.

*Very gently, very gingerly, she sponges his arm. He sets his jaw and hangs on
to himself like grim death, still keeping the gun. There is silence for a
moment as she works. We hear only the loud ticking of the kitchen clock. She
works but she is thinking. We see her catch her breath, as though summoning
her courage. She is a shade too amiable.*

MRS. MINIVER

You must be a very fine flier?

TWO SHOT

The German gives her a hard look. It is touch and go whether he will condescend to answer.

MRS. MINIVER

Is it true you brought down six British planes?

GERMAN

(*Can't resist bragging.*) Eight—

MRS. MINIVER

Eight! How did you manage that? I mean, why didn't they bring you down?

GERMAN

(*Sardonically.*) I am good flier. Also lucky. . . (*Bitterly.*) . . . until now.

MRS. MINIVER

I think you're being luckiest of all now, if you as me. (*He winces slightly with pain.*) Sorry. I'm being as gentle as I can.

GERMAN

I say—hurry—

MRS. MINIVER

I am hurrying— (*There is another silence—only the loud ticking of the clock. She finishes.*) There!—Now if I can find a nice soft cloth. (*She moves a couple of feet, to drawer of sideboard, opens drawer.*)

CLOSE-UP—MRS. MINIVER

She takes cloths from drawer. She moves the position of the clocks lightly, to look at the time. CAMERA DRAWS BACK as she returns to the German.

MRS. MINIVER
(*Proceeding to wrap a cloth around the German's arm.*) But isn't there any sort of trick to it—I mean to avoid being unlucky?

GERMAN
No trick—training—many years—

MRS. MINIVER
(*Working.*) And experience, too? It must be much more dangerous for a beginner. I suppose you've had lots of experience?

GERMAN
(*Recalling with grim satisfaction.*) Yes. I have bombed many cities—Barcelona—Warsaw—Narvik—Rotterdam—and each time we get better. Rotterdam we destroy in six minutes—

MRS. MINIVER
(*Shocked.*) Six minutes! And *thousands* of people killed. . . .

GERMAN
(*Calmly.*) Oh, yes, very many—

She stops her task.

MRS. MINIVER
Civilians—*innocent* people?

GERMAN
Not innocent. They were against us. (*She gazes at him, profoundly shocked. He says, deadly:*) Finish!

She knots the ends of the cloth. She rises. He indicates that she shall help to put the coat about his shoulders. She does so reluctantly.

MRS. MINIVER

Do listen to me—you can't go on—your arm is
poisoned—(*He moves on, ignoring her. He goes
slowly, leaning on the furniture. Her voice takes
a note of strong pleading.*) You can't escape—
they're hunting you—night and day—and even
if they don't catch you—what good can it do?
You'll lose your arm—perhaps your life—you'll
die out there? (*Insistently.*) Do you understand
what I'm saying?

*He stops, supports himself on the sink, or whatever is at hand. He turns to
face her.*

GERMAN

You want me surrender.

MRS. MINIVER

Yes.

GERMAN

Very clever—very British—thank you!

*He steels himself and walks with determination toward the door. Again he
steadies himself, a hand on the sink. Mrs. Miniver makes a little movement to
go to his aid, but checks it. After a split second the German starts for the
door again. As he reaches it, he pauses, sways and finally crashes to the
floor. The gun slides from his grasp. Mrs. Miniver looks at him for a moment,
hesitates, comes to a decision, picks up the gun and goes out swiftly to door
of dining room.*

HALL—CLOSE SHOT AT PHONE

She comes in—picks up phone.

MRS. MINIVER
(*At phone.*) The police, please—*urgent*! . . .
Police? This is Mrs. Miniver. . . . *Miniver* . . .
Starlings . . . yes. I've got that German flier—
yes, the one who escaped—in the kitchen . . .
No, I'm quite all right—he's wounded—bring a
doctor—thank you.

As she speaks:

DISSOLVE TO:

CLOSE SHOT—MRS. MINIVER

She stands, awkwardly holding the gun, at the dining-room door. She stares off, watchful, intent.

The CAMERA PANS AWAY from her to the slumped form of the German near the kitchen door. He is still out. She watches him with anxious determination. He shows signs of coming to. His eyes open. They search to floor; he rises painfully on one elbow. He speaks, his head hanging down, not looking at her.

GERMAN
My gun?

MRS. MINIVER
I have it.

GERMAN
You call police?

MRS. MINIVER
Yes. They're bringing a doctor—it's much
better.

The German makes a tremendous effort to rise. She watches him fearfully. Painfully he gets to his knees, almost to his feet. And then he crashes down again, falling to his knees, grasping a chair, bowing his head to it.

Moved by an impulse of pity, Mrs. Miniver shoves the gun behind some crockery and runs toward him. Annoyed at being helped he strives to help himself but it is with great difficulty that she gets him to a chair. He is the picture of savage despair.

MRS. MINIVER

There now—it's better—really—you'll be
wonderfully looked after in hospital—and you'll
be safe there—and the war won't last forever—

GERMAN

(*Savagely.*) No—soon we finish it! I am finished
but others come—like me— thousands!

MRS. MINIVER

How about a nice hot cup of tea?

GERMAN

(*Gasping.*) Brandy—

She goes to a cupboard, takes out glass and bottle, pours him brandy, goes to table and gives it to him. He is about to lift the glass to his lips when there comes a sound of planes overhead. Both are arrested. Mrs. Miniver looks upward. A moment of suspense . . . Then one of the fliers is heard cutting out his engine—Vin's signal. Mrs. Miniver's face lights up. She forgets for the moment to whom she is speaking.

MRS. MINIVER

That's my boy!

The sound of heavy feet is heard on the gravel path leading to the kitchen door. Mrs. Miniver crosses to the door. CAMERA FOLLOWS her, leaving the German out of scene. She opens the door and stands quietly leaning against it.

MRS. MINIVER and LADY BELDON

Even war cannot stop young people falling in love. Mrs. Miniver's son, the pilot Vin, has fallen in love with Carol (Wright), the eighteen-year-old granddaughter of the autocratic Lady Beldon (Whitty), local dowager and aristocrat. The Minivers are, of course, delighted with Carol as their future daughter-in-law and are agreeable to the marriage, even though the couple is relatively young. But this is a time of war, and who knows what each day will bring.

INT. DRAWING ROOM AT STARLINGS—DAY

Lady Beldon is standing. An erect, daunting figure in black, in a commanding position on the hearth rug. She is glancing about the tasteful room with a sort of reluctant approval.

CLOSE-UP—LADY BELDON

She says "Hm"—she takes up a rare little statuette, says again: "Hm—" Then her eyes fall on a table on her left. It is adorned solely with a vase of roses—Miniver roses? Her expression becomes grim.

LONGER SHOT

At this inopportune moment the door opens and Mrs. Miniver enters. With a nervous air of charm and friendliness, she advances.

MRS. MINIVER
(*Offering her hand.*) Ladly Beldon—this *is* nice—won't you sit down—I can recommend the sofa—(*Lady Beldon sits very stiffly.*) I think I can guess why you've come—Vin's told you his news, hasn't he?

LADY BELDON
Yes, Mrs. Miniver.

MRS. MINIVER
I hope you're as pleased as we are—

LADY BELDON

I'm afraid not. (*Indignantly.*) Why, they're *infants*! Carol's eighteen—and that boy's not twenty—

MRS. MINIVER

They *are* young, but—

LADY BELDON

I think I should tell you frankly, I hope to persuade Carol to wait—

MRS. MINIVER

You think she may change her mind?

LADY BELDON

Frankly, yes.

MRS. MINIVER

Perhaps make a better match?

LADY BELDON

There's always that possibility—

MRS. MINIVER

I suppose it's just maternal vanity, but I don't think Carol will find anyone nicer than Vin. And I don't believe she'll change her mind.

LADY BELDON

That's a matter of opinion. Her age is a matter of fact.

MRS. MINIVER

Isn't it rather a Beldon tradition—to marry young?

LADY BELDON

I don't know what you mean.

MRS. MINIVER

My daughter Judy—I don't think you've met
Judy—Judy had a composition to write on the
Crusades last week and she brought home a
book from the library—quite a small book—
called *A Friend of King Richard the Lion-
Hearted*. It was the life of an ancestor of yours.

LADY BELDON

Really, Mrs. Miniver, I fail to see—

MRS. MINIVER

It was a fascinating little book—full of stories of
the Beldon family—I got quite interested in it
myself—

LADY BELDON

(*Ironically.*) I trust you satisfied yourself that we
were worthy of the alliance.

MRS. MINIVER

Well, there *were* one or two things that rather
surprised me. Did you know the twelfth Lord
Beldon was hanged?

LADY BELDON

He was beheaded. Such things happen in the
best families—in fact usually in the best
families.

MRS. MINIVER

What interested me was the extreme youth of the
Beldon brides. This Gilbert de Beldon who went
to the Crusades married Isabel de something or
other—aged *twelve*!

LADY BELDON

My dear Mrs. Miniver, we're not in the Middle
Ages!

MRS. MINIVER

Oh, there were others! There was a Findley-
Beldon-Beldon in the seventeenth century who
eloped from Eton with a fourteen-year-old—

LADY BELDON

(*Interrupting.*) Mrs. Miniver, I didn't
come here to chatter pedigrees. I'm
old-fashioned—I believe in breeding. But that's
neither here nor there.

MRS. MINIVER

Your point is—they're both too young?

LADY BELDON

I've said so, haven't I?

MRS. MINIVER

We're at war, Lady Beldon—Vin's a flyer—

LADY BELDON

That's no excuse for rushing into an ill-
considered marriage.

MRS. MINIVER

But in war, time's so precious for the young
people. (*She looks at the old lady, wo seems to
be thinking. A light comes into Mrs. Miniver's
eye*.) How old were you when you married?

LADY BELDON

(*Taken aback.*) I?

MRS. MINIVER

It's no use telling a fib—I've looked you up.

LADY BELDON

If you've looked me up, you must know that I
was sixteen.

MRS. MINIVER

Did your parents approve?

LADY BELDON

That's beside the point—

MRS. MINIVER

Were you happy? I'm being dreadfully inquisitive?

LADY BELDON

(*Stiffly.*) Our marriage only lasted a few weeks.

MRS. MINIVER

Oh!—(*She looks contrite.*)

LADY BELDON

My husband was in the army—he was killed in action—

MRS. MINIVER

Oh, I'm *so* sorry—I didn't mean—

LADY BELDON

We married because we both knew what might happen. I don't want Carol to suffer—to suffer as I did.

MRS. MINIVER

Don't you want her to be happy—even for a few weeks as you were?

LADY BELDON

I was afraid you'd think of that . . . Not that it matters what you say—or what I say either. You know that, don't you.

MRS. MINIVER

You mean—Carol will go her own way?

LADY BELDON

She's my granddaughter—

MRS. MINIVER

Then why—er?—

LADY BELDON

Goodness knows! I was beaten before I started!

Mrs. Miniver rises impulsively, goes over to sit on the sofa besides Lady Beldon.

MRS. MINIVER

(*Charmingly—a hand on Lady Beldon's hand.*)
You don't mind terribly, do you? He *is* a nice
boy.

LADY BELDON

He's a charming boy. I see now where he gets it.
You're pretty, too. Don't wonder that wretched
Ballard named his rose after you. Not that he has
a chance of taking the Cup from me. (*Sharply.*)
Well, as long as we're going to be relatives, the
least you can do is offer me some tea!

As Mrs. Miniver jumps up smilingly:

FADE OUT

CAROL and MRS. MINIVER

One night, during one of the many Blitz raids, the Miniver house was partially damaged in one of the bombings. The dining room was destroyed and part of the upstairs. Vin's room was one of them. But that didn't stop Mrs. Miniver from fixing it up as the "home" for the newlyweds, Vin and Carol. The two young people have just come back from their honeymoon.

INT. VIN'S ROOM—REDONE

It has been damaged but remade for the newlyweds.

> **CAROL**
> (*To Mrs. Miniver.*) How sweet of you to do this—I can't think how you had the time—

> **MRS. MINIVER**
> It was a bit of a rush—but I thoroughly enjoyed myself . . .

> **CAROL**
> Thanks for the lovely room—and thanks for Vin—

> **MRS. MINIVER**
> He *is* nice, isn't he?

> **CAROL**
> I wonder if you know how much I love him—

> **MRS. MINIVER**
> (*Smiles.*) I've only to look at you—and him. (*She walks to window.*) Have you seen the view? It really is beautiful—

Carol walks over to her and together they stand in a square bay, looking across the country, the gleaming river.

> **CAROL**
> (*Dreamily.*) Yes—

MRS. MINIVER

(*Looking at her.*) You're happy?—

CAROL

(*Almost sharply.*) Of course—(*After a little pause, gravely.*) I've had a lifetime of happiness in these last two weeks . . .

MRS. MINIVER

(*With a touch of fear.*) But, Carol, it's only the beginning—

Carol turns to face her.

CAROL

Kay—I'm not afraid to face the truth—are you?

MRS. MINIVER

(*After a pause—low.*) No—

CAROL

I love him—but I know—

MRS. MINIVER

Carol!—

CAROL

(*Hard.*)—I know that I may lose him. He's young and he loves life. But he may die—let me say it—he may be killed—any day—any hour—you must have faced that in your mind—

MRS. MINIVER

(*She sits.*) Yes—I've faced it—

CAROL

Then you know that every moment is precious—
we mustn't waste time in fear— (*Sits beside
her.*) Kay, you won't hate me for saying this—

MRS. MINIVER

No, Carol—

CAROL

(*Exalted.*) I *will* be very happy—every moment
that I have him—every moment—if I must lose
him—there'll be time enough for tears —there'll
be a lifetime for tears—afterwards—(*She looks
at Mrs. Miniver.*) That's right, isn't it?

Mrs. Miniver nods her head, puts her hand on the girl's and smiles.

AN AMERICAN IN PARIS

There is a strange sort of reasoning in Hollywood that musicals are less worthy of Academy consideration than dramas. It's a form of snobbism, the same sort that perpetuates the idea that drama is more deserving of awards than comedy.

GENE KELLY

M-G-M 1951
Produced by Arthur Freed
Directed by Vincente Minnelli
Screenplay by Alan Jay Lerner from his original story

AAN: Picture, Director, Story & Screenplay, Cinematography (color), Art Airection/Set Direction (color), Costume Design (color), Editing, Scoring of a Musical Picture

AA: Picture, Story & Screenplay, Sinematography (color), Art Sirection/Set Direction, Costume Design (color), Musical Scoring
(Plus a special award to Gene Kelly for choreography)

CAST
Gene Kelly, Oscar Levant, Nina Foch, Leslie Caron, Georges Guétary

Brodway Melody was a silent picture in which the musical numbers were recorded with that new gimmick, *sound. The Great Ziegfeld* was essentially a dramatic picture with lavish production numbers interpolated to show Ziggy's opulent production style and eye; but the songs had nothing to do with advancing either character or plot. And *Going My Way* was a sentimental comedy with songs plugged in because the audience expected Bing Crosby to sing, and they had hired a boys' choir that had to be used, and they had also signed Rise Stevens. So, *An American in Paris* was the first bona fide *musical* to win the Best Picture statuette. Within the next 20 years there were five other musicals to join it in the winner's circle (and at least two other musicals that shoud have been there). *Oliver*, 1968, however, was the last musical to win the top trophy.

Oddly, enough, *An American in Paris* is not a musical with an "original" score written directly for it's screenplay. It is what is referred to as a "catalogue" musical. The script for the movie was written around a series of songs that had been written previously for any number of disparate productions or uses. It was up to the screenwriter to make songs "work" as if they were written for this story.

Jerry Mulligan (Kelly) is a happy-go-lucky, expatriate American living the carefree, bohemian life of a struggling painter in Paris. He hasn't got a sou in his pocket, but what does he care? He's got a smile on his face, a song in his throat, and a dance in his feet. And he doesn't even have to worry about where his next breakfast comes from: he's the *one* American every Parisian loves. Keep in mind that this is Gershwin, Gershwin, and Lerner—*not* Puccini!

One sunny afternoon—it never rains in Paris in musical comedy—Jerry is spotted by a pretty, wealthy American woman, Milo (Foch), who seems interested in his painting, but is actually more interested in *him*. Jerry, though, is smitten with a Parisian gamine (Caron), who just happens to be the steady of one of his new friends, a Parisian music hall star, Henri [Guétary]). Jerry is torn between the two women. Should he go with the rich one and partake of all the advantages—both professionally and personally—that she can provide him? Or should he fight for the girl he really loves, be happy, and let the palette of the art critics paint his future? The only way he can express his frustration is in a huge dream ballet (that took twenty-five percent of the the the film's budget to produce). This is musical comedy, folks, so was the answer ever in doubt?

MILO and JERRY

Milo was driving by in her limo earlier in the day and just happened to see Jerry on the sidewalk hawking his unsold and undiscovered paintings. Milo bought a couple of the canvasses, and expressed great interest in his work. She also invited Jerry back to her hotel suite that same night on the pretext of giving a party; she says there is an extra girl. Jerry, delighted at the attention to his work, naive enough to think her interest is solely professional, and hungry enough for a free meal, accepts Milo's invitation.

INT. MILO'S SUITE—NIGHT

Jerry is lolling in a comfortable chair. He apparently has been waiting for some time. Jerry lights a cigarette. He crosses and looks down at his pictures for a moment. He turns quickly as Milo enters. She has on a short evening dress. It's an off-the-shoulder model—way off. She looks quite ravishing.

MILO
Good evening. I'm sorry I'm late.

She extends her hand. He is obviously taken with the way she looks. He shakes her hand.

JERRY

Good evening.

MILO

The moment I went in to dress, the phone started ringing like a steeple on Sunday. Would you like a short one before dinner?

JERRY

Fine.

He doesn't take his eyes off her. She goes to a piece of furniture that when opened turns out to be a pseudo-bar and prepares "two short ones."

MILO

(*As she goes.*) I've never seen so many Americans in Paris before. The Champs-Élysées is like Main Street.

JERRY

Do you live here all the time?

MILO

Oh, I usually go home to Baltimore for Thanksgiving and Christmas. (*She turns to him with the drinks.*)

JERRY

That's quite a dress you almost have on.

MILO

(*Smiles.*) Thank you. (*She hands him his glass.*)

JERRY

What holds it up?

MILO
Modesty. Cheers.

JERRY
Cheers.

They each sip.

JERRY
So this is a formal brawl after all.

MILO
Why do you think that?

JERRY
The more formal a party is, the less you have to wear.

MILO
(*Laughing lightly.*) No. You're wrong. It's most informal.

She sits.

JERRY
Where is everybody?

MILO
They're all here.

JERRY
(*He sits opposite her.*) Downstairs?

MILO
No. Here. In this room.

JERRY
(*The dawn breaking slowly.*) What about that extra girl?

MILO

That's me.

JERRY

(*With seeming good nature.*) Oh! You mean the party is just you and me?

MILO

(*Nodding with a faint smile of self admiration.*) That's right.

JERRY

It's kind of a little joke, isn't it?

MILO

In a way.

He takes some bills out of his pocket and puts them on the table.

JERRY

Here's your dough back, lady. Now I'll take my pictures and get along.

He crosses and picks them up. Milo is a bit taken aback and then recovers her poise quickly.

MILO

Wait a minute!

JERRY

Wait, my foot! You must be out of your mink-lined head. I know I need money, but I don't need it this badly. If you're hard up for companionship, they have guys in Paris who do that kind of thing for a living. Call one of them.

He starts to go. Milo breaks into laughter. He stops, looks at her furiously.

JERRY

What's so funny?

MILO

You're so righteous. (*She goes to him.*)
Now stop defending your honor so assiduously
and listen a moment. I don't need a paid escort.
I'm not even trying to rob you of your precious
male initiative. I'm simply interested in your
work. And I want to get to know you better. Is
that such a crime?

JERRY

It sure is a roundabout way to do it.

He is calming down a bit.

MILO

(*A bit sheepishly.*) Would you have accepted a
normal invitation?

JERRY

No.

*She puts a hand on his arm. She is much softer now, softer than she has
hitherto been.*

MILO

I want to help you. I think you have a great deal
of talent. It doesn't hurt to have someone rooting
for you, does it?

JERRY

(*After a pause, seriously.*) It'll be the first time
anybody did.

MILO

Then let me. Please.

*She lightly takes the picture from under his arm. He walks away from her. He
is deep in thought. Without turning, he says, after a moment:*

JERRY

How's the food downstairs?

MILO

(*Restraining her delight.*) Very good.

JERRY

And probably very expensive.

MILO

Would it embarrass you if I signed the check?

JERRY

Yes. Let's go some place I can afford.

MILO

How about the Café Flodair in Montparnasse?
I feel like some "jazz hot"—and it's not
expensive.

JERRY

It better not be. I want to show a little profit at
the end of this day.

JERRY and LISE

At the Café Flodair in Montparnasse, Jerry first sighted the girl of his
dreams—or at least the girl that attracted him instantly: Lise. He finds out
where she works, a parfumery, and bothers her there until she agrees to meet
him at a local sidewalk café. He is waiting anxiously for her—impatient for
her to arrive and fearful that she will not show up. But she does. He is just as
attractive to her; and he intrigues her. So then, what is more irresistible to a
proper, engaged girl than a clandestine meeting with a vivacious, handsome
near-stranger? It's a very daring thing for a proper girl to do—and just a little
bit naughty, isn't it?

LISE WALKING TOWARD THE CAFÉ

Ahead, she sees Jerry pacing slowly up and down. He turns when he sees her. They approach each other hesitantly. Lise seems nervous: Almost like a girl's first date after six years in a convent. Even Jerry doesn't have his usual aplomb.

A theme of the "American in Paris" is heard underneath.

JERRY
(*Staring at her for a moment first.*) Hello. . . .

LISE
(*Almost frightened.*) Hello. . . .

She looks around discreetly.

JERRY
(*After a long pause.*) Would . . . would you like a drink?

LISE
Thank you.

He leads her to a table on the sidewalk and helps her sit. The Café Bel-Ami is a typical small café. The river Seine flows by before them. In the middle of the river is the Ile de St.-Louis. Rising proudly on the Ile is Notre-Dame.

Jerry sits down opposite her. He tries to be conversational.

JERRY
I wasn't sure you'd come. (*She doesn't answer. Just looks around cautiously.*) I thought maybe you'd just said yes to get rid of me. (*She smiles weakly.*) Not that it would have. What would you like?

LISE
(*She sees a man looking at her and turns her back to him quickly.*) I. . . . Would you mind if we didn't sit here?

JERRY
No.

She rises quickly and walks away from the café. Jerry rises and looks after her. Jerry walks to Lise.

ALONG THE RIVER

Jerry catches up with her and they walk for a moment in silence.

LISE
(*Without looking at him.*) I'm sorry.

JERRY
(*Easily.*) For what? I didn't feel much like sitting there anyhow. (*She gives him a quick look of appreciation.*) Let's walk along the river.

LISE
(*A little more comfortable.*) All right.

They walk for a moment in silence.

JERRY
There's a spot along here I have a big thing for. One of these days I'm going to paint it.

LISE
(*With mild interest.*) You're a painter?

JERRY
Hmmmph.

LISE
You don't look like a painter.

JERRY

There are those, dear lady, who will tell you I don't paint like one either. But it doesn't bother me. Discouragement stimulates me.

LISE

(*Smiling a little.*) That much about you I know.

JERRY

Yes, you do, don't you? (*He stops, she does too.*) But mark me well. One day the world will ring with the name of Mulligan. Picasso will be remembered as the forerunner of Mulligan. That tree will be famous because it was painted by Mulligan.

They walk on. She is quite amused.

LISE

And when will this golden age of art be?

JERRY

(*With exaggerated sagacity.*) It's hard to say. Civilization has a natural resistance against improving itself. It might take quite awhile. Quite awhile. (*They walk for a moment in silence.*) How do you feel now?

LISE

Why?

JERRY

You were acting like the police were after you.

LISE

I was, wasn't I?

JERRY

Why? (*She doesn't answer.*) Never mind. Don't try and think up what to tell me. I don't have to know. It's our business.

They walk for a moment. She slips her arm through his. He notices it. They pass a man selling chestnuts.

JERRY

Would you like some chestnuts?

LISE

Thank you.

He gives the man some coins and takes two bags. He hands her one and they continue walking.

LISE

I couldn't eat a whole bag myself.

JERRY

Try. The night is young. Let's live dangerously.

He looks at her and winks. She smiles.

A STONE BENCH OVERLOOKING A BUSY QUAI

Several boats are preparing to leave. Others are coming in. Others are going around the island.

First seen is an empty bag of chestnuts lying on the bench. Next to the bag Jerry and Lise. She has a few chestnuts in her hand. She is eating them.

JERRY

(*Moving slowly towards her.*) Saturday night is the big night back home. No school. No work. And by the time you get home, no money.

LISE

(*Oblivious to his "moving in."*) And Sunday? Is Sunday nice in America?

JERRY

In America everybody catches cold on Sunday.

LISE

Did you?

JERRY

Sometimes. (*He has his arm around the back of her resting on the bench.*) What about you? Aren't you sick of the life and times of Mulligan?

LISE

(*Finishing the last one.*) I'd rather listen to you. I don't like to talk about myself.

JERRY

You're going to have to get over that.

LISE

Why?

She looks at him.

JERRY

(*His face not far from hers.*) Because with a binding like you've got, people are going to want to know what's in the book.

LISE

(*A little breathlessly.*) What . . . what does that mean?

JERRY

Primarily it means you're a very beautiful girl.

LISE

(*Sincerely.*) I am?

JERRY

Yes, you are.

LISE

(*Also sincerely.*) How do you know?

JERRY

I heard it on the radio.

He leans a little forward as if to kiss her. She draws away more at what he said than at what he is doing.

LISE

You're making fun with me.

JERRY

Doesn't everybody tell you?

LISE

I haven't been out with many people. And they're always friends.

JERRY

Honey, believe me, I'm no enemy.

LISE

(*Looking out at a particular boat about to shove off—the captain is standing with one foot on the boat, one on the landing.*) The captain is getting ready to sail.

JERRY

(*In her ear.*) Good for him. Lise, I don't know whether you're really a girl of mystery or just a still water that doesn't run deep, but there's one thing I can tell you: If I'd been around sooner you'd know by now you're beautiful. (*He leans forward to kiss her. She rises and stands away from him. He goes to her—sincerely*) And I'm not making fun "with you."

SONG: "I'VE GOT A CRUSH ON YOU"

ANOTHER ANGLE AT THE QUAI—CLOSE SHOT—LISE AND JERRY.

LISE

(*Suddenly.*) What time is it?

JERRY

(*Looking at his wristwatch.*) Eleven o'clock.

LISE

(*Jumping up.*) Eleven o'clock! I have to go!

JERRY

Where?

LISE

I have to.

He holds her. They're both standing.

JERRY

Wait a minute. When will I see you again?

LISE

I don't know.

JERRY

Lise, we have to see each other again.

LISE

(*Seriously.*) Yes, we do. Don't we?

JERRY

Tomorrow night?

LISE

I can't. How about lunch?

JERRY

No. I tell you. Saturday morning I'm at the
Ecole des Beaux Arts. I'm finished at noon. Can
you meet me there?

LISE

Saturday? Yes. I'll meet you.

*She moves to go. He holds her. He kisses her quickly. She leaves his arms
and walks away quickly. He stands looking after her.*

GIGI

It has the sureness expected when a group of the most sophisticated talents are able to work together on material entirely suited to them.

PENELOPE HOUSTON

M-G-M 1958
Produced by Arthur Freed
Directed by Vincente Minnelli
Screenplay by Alan Jay Lerner from the story by Collette

AAN: picture, director, writing (screenplay based on material from
another medium), cinematography (color),
art direction/set direction (color), song, scoring of a musical,
costume design, editing

AA: picture, director, screenplay, cinematography (color), art direction/set
direction (color), song, scoring of a musical picture, costume design,
editing , (plus a special award to Maurice Chevalier)

CAST
Leslie caron, Louis Jourdan, Maurice Chevalier, Hermione Gingold,
Isabel Jeans, Jacques Bergerac, Eva Gabor, John Abbott

The second musical to win the Best Picture Oscar is such an advance over the first that it is a small miracle of picturization and sophistication. What is even more amazing is that the screenplay, director, and producer of *An American in Paris* were the same trio that created *Gigi*. This time they added a lush, melodic score by Frederick Lowe and Alan Jay Lerner contributed his own sophisticated lyrics. Nearly everything about *Gigi* works on the screen. It is funny, touching, romantic, beautiful to look at, and the songs perform the function songs in the best of book musicals do: they further either the plot or the character, or both at the same time. And the legendary picturization and compostion for which Vincente Minnelli was noted has never been more telling. The result is one of the most luscious jewels in anybody's treasure box—an exquisite emerald with that miracle, the dancing flame of elusive blue in its center, which only the best emeralds possess, as Gigi's Aunt Alicia would describe it.

If you like opulantly produced, costumed, romantic musical comedies, then you are a sucker for *Gigi*. If you don't, then nothing that can be said in defense of the movie will sway you. However, the Academy liked *Gigi* well enough to give it nine nominations, and then give it nine awards. This is a record held by only two other films. In 1934, *It Happened One Night* was nominated for five Oscars, and it won five. *Gigi* was the second film in the Academy's history to win every Oscar for which it was nominated. And it was not until 1987 when *The Last Emperor* received nine nominations and then won nine Oscars was the feat repeated. Strangely enough, neither *Gigi* nor *The Last Emperor* could rope a nomination in any of the acting categories.

Gigi is based on a novel by the French writer Collette. It's the story of a teenage girl growing up in La Belle Epoque Paris around the turn of the century. She attracts the attention of a wealthly playboy, Gaston LaChaille, who suddenly discovers that he has fallen in love with her. He proposes to "take care of her—beautifully."Since Gigi comes from a family of professional courtesans, this should be no problem. But Gigi has other ideas, and she rejects Gaston's offer. This sends shock waves through both Gigi's family and Gaston.

GIGI AND AUNT ALICIA

Every week, in the afternoon after school, the exhuberant teenage Gigi has to go to her wealthy and eccentric great-aunt Alicia for another set of "lessons." Gigi is not quite sure what these lessons are for, or all about, or why she has to take them, but she does. Her Grandmama has said she has to take them, and after all Aunt Alicia is a member of the family. Surely these lessons are meant to better her in some way, Gigi thinks. So, as a good granddaugter and great-niece, she endures them and tries her best to master each lesson. Even though she doesn't understand why.

INT. AUNT ALICIA'S APARTMENT—DAY

Aunt Alicia is waiting, quite proper a society matron, for Gigi. Gigi enters the apartment, slamming the door behind her. Aunt Alicia gives a brief headshake of hopelessness as Gigi runs into the room.

AUNT ALICIA
Slowly, Gigi. Slowly. The racing season is
over.

Gigi slows down.

GIGI
Good day, Aunt Alicia.

Aunt Alicia (indicating the dining room).

GIGI
Yes, Aunt Alicia.

They move toward the dining room.

AUNT ALICIA
Today you will learn to eat ortolans.

THE DINING ROOM

Charles, the butler, helps Aunt Alicia into her chair. Gigi is about to sit then remembers to wait until Aunt Alicia is seated.

GIGI
(*During the above.*) What are ortolans, Aunt Alicia?

AUNT ALICIA
Exquisite little birds. Most people atack them like cannibals. You will learn to eat them properly. Bad table manners, my dear Gigi, have broken up more households than infidelity.

Charles serves. The ortolans are indeed tiny. Gigi looks at them hopelessly.

AUNT ALICIA
Did you work hard in school? What did you study?

GIGI
History. The Spanish Inquisition

AUNT ALICIA

How depressing. What else?

GIGI

English.

AUNT ALICIA

I suppose you must. They refuse to learn
French. Who are your friends? Ortolans
should be cut in two with a quick stroke of the
knife and no grating of the blade on the plate.
Bite up each half. The bones don't matter. Go
on eating while you answer my questions, but
don't talk with your mouth full. You must
manage it. If I can, you can. What friends have
you made?

*Aunt Alicia artfully slips the birds into her mouth and they seem
miraculously to melt. With Gigi, every bone is heard angonizingly
breaking.*

GIGI

None. Grandmama won't let me have tea with
the families of my school friends.

AUNT ALICIA

She is quite right. Apart from that, there is no
one who follows you, no little grocery boy
hanging around your shirts? No older man? I
warn you, I shall know at once if you lie.

GIGI

Oh, no, Aunt Alicia. There is no one. I am
always on my own. But why does Grandmama
stop me from accepting invitations?

AUNT ALICIA

She is right, for once. You would only be
invited by ordinary people.

GIGI

What about us? Aren't we ordinary people?

AUNT ALICIA

No.

GIGI

Why are we different?

AUNT ALICIA

They have weak heads and careless bodies.
Besides, they are married. But I don't think
you would understand.

GIGI

And we don't marry? Is that it?

AUNT ALICIA

Marriage is not forbidden to us. Instead of
getting married "at once," it sometimes
happens that we get married "at last." But
enough. We must finish lunch and get on to
your jewelry lesson.

THE ROOM

*Gigi and Aunt Alicia are emerging from the dining room. Aunt Alicia
leads her to a table upon which is a jewelry box. They seat themselves.*

AUNT ALICIA

Without knowledge of jewelry, my dear Gigi, a
woman is lost. Do you remember Madam
Dumard who was here the other day?

GIGI

Yes.

AUNT ALICIA

Did you notice the string of black pearls
around her throat?

GIGI

Oh, yes. They were beautiful.

AUNT ALICIA

Dipped.

GIGI

Dipped?

AUNT ALICIA

Dipped. A present from the man she loves
whose love is obviously beginning to cool and
the poor thing doesn't know it. It's just a
matter of time now. Let's see what you
remember. (*Holds up a diamond.*) What's
this?

GIGI

A . . . marquise diamond.

AUNT ALICIA

A marquise-*shaped* diamond. (*Holds up
another.*) And this?

GIGI

(*Thinks.*) That . . . is . . . a . . . topaz.

AUNT ALICIA

(*Shrieks, horrified.*) A topaz amongst my
jewels! Are you mad? It's a yellow diamond of
the first quality. You'll have to go a long way
to see one like it. (*She picks up another.*)
This?

GIGI
An emerald. How beautiful!

AUNT ALICIA
(*In reverent, hushed tones.*) Do you see that blue flame darting about in the depths of the green light? Only the most beautiful emeralds contain that miracle of elusive blue.

GIGI
Who gave it to you, Aunt?

AUNT ALICIA
A king.

GIGI
A great king.

AUNT ALICIA
No. A little one. Great kings do not give very large stones.

GIGI
Why not?

AUNT ALICIA
In my opinion it's because they don't feel they have to.

GIGI
Who does give the valuable jewels?

AUNT ALICIA
Who? The shy and the proud. And the social climbers because they think it's a sign of culture. But it doesn't matter who gives them, as long as you never wear anything second-rate. Wait for the first-class jewels, Gigi. Hold onto your ideals.

GIGI

What if I don't get any?

AUNT ALICIA

Well, then it can't be helped. But rather than wear a wretched little diamond full of flaws, wear a simple, inexpensive ring. Then you can always say it's a memento you wouldn't part with for the world. Now, let's go over it again. There's the white, the blue-white, the yellow or the pick diamond; the ruby, if you can be sure of it; the sapphire, if it comes from Kashmir; the emerald— which you know, and—these are real pearls.

GIGI

(*Sitting back with a sigh.*) Oh.

AUNT ALICIA

What?

GIGI

I'll never remember all of this.

AUNT ALICIA

You'll have to. (*She looks at her closely.*) Come around here, Gigi.

Gigi comes around and stands in front of her.

AUNT ALICIA

Open your mouth. (*Gigi does. Aunt Alicia examines Gigi's teeth*) With teeth like that I could have devoured all Paris and most of Europe. (*She laughs.*) But I can't complain. I had a good bite of it. (*Aunt Alicia rubs Gigi's cheek*) Tell you grandmama to get you some astringent lotion. You don't use powder, do you?

GIGI

No. Grandmama won't let me.

AUNT ALICIA

I should hope not. You have an impossible
nose, a nondescript mouth; your cheekbones
are too high. But we can do something with
the rest of you. Your teeth, your eyes and
eyelashes, your hair. We can, and we will.
Remind me, you must learn to choose cigars.

She starts for the door.

GIGI

But, Aunt Alicia, I don't smoke cigars!

AUNT ALICIA

Of course you dont smoke cigars, but a man
does. Everything I teach you has a good
reason. Love, my dear Gigi, is a thing of
beauty, like a work of art. And like a work of
art, it's created by artists. The greater the artist,
the greater the art. And what makes an artist?

GIGI

(*Wanly.*) Cigars and jewelry.

AUNT ALICIA

Gigi, you are from another planet. Get on with
your work.

She sweeps out. Gigi starts picking up the jewels, one at a time.

GIGI, GASTON, AND GRANDMA

Up to now the wealthy, handsome, and worldly Gaston LaChaille has been like an experienced big brother or doting uncle to the teenage Gigi. He brings her caramels and plays cards with her on Sunday afternoons. He takes her for sweet drinks at the Palace of Ice and for rides in his carriage in Bois de Bologne. He takes Gigi and her Grandmama to the beach because Gigi has never been there before.

But Gigi has been changing from an awkward girl to being on the verge of a young lady. Gigi is not aware of this, but Aunt Alicia is. She has also been aware of the "signals" Gaston's actions have been sending since he has been enjoying the company of this young girl. And Aunt Alicia has made sure Grandmama understands. Gaston and Gigi, however, at this point, consider themselves still innocent friends to one another. To Aunt Alicia and Grandmama, though, the time has come to define the association and relationship in different terms.

INT. LIVING ROOM—GIGI'S AND GRANDMAMA'S APARTMENT

GASTON

I've decided your new dress may not be as
bad as all that. I didn't see it properly, and
perhaps I was a bit cruel.

Gaston hands her a box of caramels. Gigi takes one, laughing happily.

GASTON

And to prove it, I'll take you for a drive in it
and we'll have tea at the Reservoirs in
Versailles. Would you like to?

GIGI

(*Overcome with joy.*) I'd love it! Grandmama,
Gaston wants to take me to the Reservoirs.

Grandmama joins Gigi and Gaston in the living room.

GRANDMAMA

You've come back, Gaston? How tolerant
you are.

GASTON

(*Embarrassed.*) I hadn't really gone.

GIGI

Grandmama, we're going to have tea at the
Reservoirs.

GRANDMAMA

(*With firmness.*) No, you're not. I'm sorry,
Gaston.

GASTON

Hmph? How do you mean?

GIGI

(*Begins to cry.*) Grandmama, please.

GRANDMAMA

Gigi, go to your room for a minute. I have to
talk to Gaston about something.

GIGI

No, Grandmama.

Grandmama pushes her out of the door.

GRANDMAMA

Do as you're told.

Gigi exits.

GASTON

Well, Mamita, what does this mean? Something
has changed here lately. I can feel it.

GRANDMAMA

Sit down, dear Gaston.

Gaston sits down and takes a caramel. Grandmama sits opposite him.

GRANDMAMA

Gaston, you know my friendship for you. My friendship and my gratitude. But I mustn't forget my duty. Gigi's mother, as you know, has neither the time nor the mind to take care of her. And Gigi isn't just another girl. She's special.

GASTON

Of course.

GRANDMAMA

For years you've been giving her candies and trinkets. She adores you. And now you want to take her in your automobile to the Reservoirs for tea. If it were you and I, I would say take Gigi wherever you want. I would trust her with you anywhere. But there are others, Gaston. You are known everywhere. For a woman to go out with you alone, especially now . . . with the eyes of Paris upon you . . . well. . . .

GASTON

(*Interrupts.*) Are you trying to make me believe that if Gigi goes out with me she'll be compromised? (*He laughs sarcastically.*) A slip of a girl, a little brat no one knows, no one notices.

GRANDMAMA

(*Very pointedly.*) Let's say then that she'd be labelled. No matter where you go your presence is noticed. A young girl who goes out with you is no longer an ordinary young girl, not even a respectable young girl. Gigi, above all, must not cease to be an ordinary young girl, at least not in that respect.

GASTON

Mamita, this is absurd.

GRANDMAMA

So far as you are concerned, it would be just
another news item. But in this case, I wouldn't
have the heart to laugh about it when I read it
in the paper.

GASTON

(*Angrily.*) Mamita, this is all too ridiculous to
discuss any further. I don't want to contradict
you and I don't want to argue about it. If you
feel you are protecting Gigi from some cruel
fate, that's your affair.

GRANDMAMA

I understand responsibility to Gigi better than
you, Gaston. I'll do all I can to entrust her
only to a man who'll be able to say: I'll take
care of her and I'll answer for her future.

There is a loaded silence.

GRANDMAMA

Now, could I make you some camomile tea,
Gaston?

GASTON

No, thank you. I have an appointment and I
am late already.

He strides to the door. Then stops and turns for a farewell address.

GASTON

But forgive me if I wonder, Madame, whom
you are keeping her for! Some underpaid
bank clerk who'll marry her and give her four
children in three years?

GRANDMAMA

Please, Gaston, don't upset yourself.

GASTON

To see her married in white in some dingey
little church to a plumber who'll give her
nothing but a worthless name and the squalor
of good intentions? Very well, Madame, if
that's your ambition, inflict your misery in
the name of respectability. I pity you. I pity
you all.

He exits grandly.

GIGI, GASTON, AND GRANDMA

A great revelation has hit Gaston, subtlely, rather like being serenaded by
the booming of a bass drum. *He is in love with this blossoming young
lady, Gigi!* (Surprise, surprise, folks. Who in the audience missed the
coming of that one?) And being the honorable man of the world that he
is, he takes Grandmama and Aunt Alicia up on their offer and in all
civilized fashsion offers terms for Gigi's care and future as his mistress.
To the older women, who have had experience in this sort of life, this is
reasonable. But Gigi is from another generation, with other ideals and
other values.

INT. LIVING ROOM—GIGI'S APARTMENT—NIGHT

*The doorbell sounds. Gigi comes out of her bedroom, goes to the front
door, opens it. It is Gaston. He has flowers in his hand.*

GIGI

Hello, Gaston.

GASTON

(*Putting his hat and cane away.*) Good
evening, Gigi.

*They walk into the living room. They bump into each other. There is an
embarrassed silence.*

GASTON

Here. (*He hands her the flowers.*)

GIGI

(*Putting flowers on the table.*) Thank you, Gaston.

She sits down on the sofa.

GIGI

Sit down, Gaston. (*She indicates for him to sit next to her.*) I'm sorry I didn't have time to get dressed. Not like you. You look beautiful.

GASTON

(*Sitting next to her—gently.*) What's the matter, Gigi? What's wrong? You know why I'm here.

GIGI

(Without looking at him.) I know.

GASTON

Do you want to, or don't you?

GIGI

(*Softly.*) I don't want to. I really don't know what *you* want. You said to Grandmama that I. . . .

GASTON

(*Interrupting.*) I know what I told your grandmother. . . . You don't have to repeat it. Just tell me simply what you *don't* want and tell me what you *do* want.

GIGI

Do you mean that?

GASTON

Of course I do.

GIGI

Well, Gaston, you told Grandmama you want
to take care of me.

GASTON

To take care of you beautifully.

GIGI

Beautifully. That is, if I like it. They have
pounded into me that I am backward for my
age, but I know very well what all this means.
To take care of me beautifully means I should
go away from here with you and that I should
sleep in your bed.

GASTON

(*Shocked and sad.*) Please, Gigi, I beg you.
You embarrass me.

GIGI

You weren't embarrassed to talk to
Grandmama about it. And Grandmama wasn't
embarrassed to talk to me about it. But I know
more than she told me. I know very well that
taking care of me means that my photograph
will be in the papers. I'll go to the Riviera and
to the races at Deauville. When we have a fight,
it will be in the columns the next day. When
you throw me over once and for all, as you did
Ynez des Cevennes when you'd had enough
of her.

GASTON

How do you know about that? Who's been
filling your head with all these old stories?

GIGI

Why shouldn't I know? You're world famous.
I know about the woman who stole money
from you, the American who wanted you to
marry her, the Comtesse who wanted to shoot
you. . . . I know what everybody knows.

GASTON

(*Gently.*) These aren't the things we have to
talk about together, Gigi. That's all in the past.
Over and done with.

GIGI

Of course, Gaston. Until it begins again. It's
not your fault you're world famous. It's just
. . . that I haven't got a world famous sort of
nature. When it's over Monsieur Lachaille
goes away with another lady. And I have only
to go into another gentleman's bed. I don't
want to. I'm not changeable. It won't do for
me. (*She turns away from him.*) Grandmama
and Aunt Alicia are on your side, but this
concerns me a little, too, and I think I should
have something to say about it. And what I say
is: It won't work. It won't work.

*She begings to cry. Gaston is at a lost what to do. He makes a move as if
to put his arm around her, then stops. He rises and paces a bit.*

GASTON

(*Finally.*) Gigi, are you just trying to find a
way to tell me that I don't please you . . . that
you don't like me?

GIGI

(*Passionately.*) Oh, no, Gaston. I *do* like you.
I'm always happy when I'm with you.
Couldn't we go on as we are, only maybe
seeing each other more often? No one will
think anything of it, since you're a friend of
the family. You will bring licorice and
caramels, and champagne on my birthday.
And on Sunday we'll have an extra special
game of cards. Wouldn't that be a nice little
life?

GASTON

(*Sitting next to her tenderly.*) A wonderful
little life, Gigi. Except that you forget one
thing. I'm in love with you.

GIGI

(*Bewildered.*) You never told me.

GASTON

I haven't known very long. I discovered it
when I was away form you. In Monte Carlo.

GIGI

(*In smouldering rage.*) Oh, you are a wicked
man! You're in love with me and you want
to drag me into a life that will make me
suffer . . . !

She begins to sob. Gaston is alarmed.

GIGI

You're in love with me and you think nothing
of exposing me to all sorts of terrible
adventures, ending in separation, quarrels,
pistol shots, Sandomirs and poison.

Gigi is now beyond control. Gaston is half frightened, half desperate.

GASTON
No, Gigi, no. Listen to me.

GIGI
(*Screaming.*) I would never have believed it of
you, Gaston! Never! Never!

Grandmama enters from the other room.

GRANDMAMA
What's the matter? What's happened?

GASTON
(*Blaming Grandmama.*) She doesn't seem to
want to.

GRANDMAMA
She doesn't want to! What do you mean?

GASTON
I mean she doesn't want to.

GRANDMAMA
Gigi! Are you going out of your mind?! (*To
Gaston.*) Gaston, as God is my witness, I
explained everything to her. Believe me, I did.

*Gaston, infuriated, strides to the door. Then stops and turns for another
farewell address.*

GASTON
You explained too much. You've trained this
child to know nothing but the sordid and the
vulgar. But what about kindness, sweetness,
benevolence? What of the tender heart bulging
with generosity? These things exist too,
Madame. Or have you never heard of them?

He exits grandly, slamming the door behind him.

GASTON AND HONORE

What is the world coming to? The young woman with whom he is in love turns down his offers of being a kept woman. She scorned him because he said he loves her and wants to keep her. Gaston made an honest, cavalier offer of love to a mistress before any emotional commitment was exchanged—a pure business offer—and it's turned down! And then she accuses him of all sorts of shameful things, confusing and frustrating the hell out of him. She tells Gaston, "You say you love me and yet you propose to do this awful thing to me!" What awful thing? What is this younger generation coming to? Gaston LaChaille is at the end of one great tether and he doesn't know what to do, he just knows he's got to do something or explode. Never has this happened to him before. Luckily, he finds the one person who can give him the advice he needs: his uncle, Honore LaChaille, man of the world and understander of women.

EXT. SIDEWALK CAFE—DAY

Honore is having a little snack, consisting of salad, cheese, and wine. Gaston comes marching down the street to his table and seats himself. Honore goes right on eating.

GASTON
I tell you, Uncle, Europe is breeding a
generation of vandals and ingrates. Children
are coming into the world with ice-covered
souls and hatchets in their hands, and before
they have finished, they'll smash everything
beautiful and decent.

HONORE
(*Casually.*) Have a piece of cheese.

GASTON
No, thank you. I envy you, Uncle. I envy
you your age. For you it was different.
You've been clean and good and it's been
appreciated. But not any more. It's over.
All over.

HONORE
I'm sorry to hear it. A little salad?

GASTON

No, thank you. Imagine this, if you can: here's a girl, living in a moldy apartment, decaying walls, worm-ridden furniture, surrounded by filth. . . .

HONORE

You're ruining my lunch.

GASTON

Nothing to look forward to but abject poverty. My heart was touched. I wanted to help her. I offered her everything: a house, a car, servants, clothes—and me.

HONORE

And? . . .

GASTON

She turned me down.

HONORE

Turned you down? It's impossible.

GASTON

It isn't at all impossible. It just happened.

HONORE

Obviously that disgusting apartment she lives in has driven her mad.

GASTON

Her grandmother was delighted, but. . . .

HONORE

Grandmother?

GASTON

Yes, Mamita.

Honore is seriously surprised.

GASTON

But Gigi, no! She turned me down. I was
refused, rejected, rebuffed, repudiated.

HONORE

(*Thoughtfully—understanding.*) Well, they're
a very peculiar family with very peculiar ideas.
I negotiated with them myself once. With me,
one casual bit of grazing in another pasture
and the gate was slammed behind me. What
did you do when she turned you down?

GASTON

I left immediately.

HONORE

Bravo. The absolutely right thing to do.

GASTON

Of course.

HONORE

And when she sends for you, which you
realize she will. . . .

GASTON

(*Not realizing it at all.*) I know she will.

HONORE

This is plainly a maneuver for better terms.
Don't you go back.

GASTON

Go back? Why, I wouldn't go back for
anything in the world. Do you think I
would? . . .

HONORE

After all, you behaved like a perfect
gentleman.

GASTON

(*Righteously.*) There's no question about it.

HONORE

You made your offer in good faith, before any
emotional advance. An act of the purest
chivalry.

GASTON

I wouldn't know how to do it any other way.

HONORE

And if she doesn't appreciate the nobility of
your conduct, if she uses the beauty of your
nature as a weapon for bargaining, then she's
obviously not worth the chivalry *or* the
nobility. It's no one's fault. You're just too
good for her. Do you know how long it will
take you to forget her?

GASTON

Oh, I should say. . . .

HONORE

By tomorrow noon at the latest. Now why
don't you consult your little book and meet
me at Maxim's tonight?

GASTON

Splendid idea.

HONORE

I would suggest a redhead. Try Michele. I saw
her last night and she looked heavenly.

GASTON

I'll call her at once.

HONORE

You should. She doesn't have many good
years left. See you at nine?

GASTON

(*Rising.*) Nine sharp. Adieu, Uncle.

HONORE

Adieu, my boy.

Gaston walks happily down the street.

BEN-HUR

MGM's future rides on the success or failure of Ben-Hur.

MIKE CONNOLLY

A major motion picture phenomenon.

FILMS IN REVIEW

M-G-M 1959
Produced by Sam Zimbalist
Directed by William Wyler
Screenplay by Karl Tunberg with contributions from Christopher fry,
Maxwell Anderson, S. N. Behrman, and Gore Vidal,
from the novel by Lew Wallace

AAN: picture, director, actor (Charlton Heston), supporting actor
(Hugh Griffith), writing (screenplay based on, material from another
medium), cinematography (color), art direction/set decoration (color), sound,
musical score, costume design (color), editing, special effects

AA: picture, director, actor, supporting actor, cinematography (color),
art direction/set decoration (color), sound, musical score,
costume design (color), editing, special effects

CAST
Charlton Heston, Haya Haraeet, Jack Hawkins, Stephen Boyd,
Hugh Griffith, Martha Scott, Sam Jaffe, Cathy O'Donnell, Finlay Curie,
Frank Thring, Terence Longdon, André Morell, George Relph

*B*en-Hur has been before the cameras three times. First in 1907 as a one-reeler, and then in 1926 in a silent spectacular costing $4 million, but with performances by Ramon Navarro and Francis X. Bushman that still intrigue today; and then as a $15 million talkie in 1959 which has a 3 hour and 32 minute playing time, of which fifteen minutes is one chariot race. (But what a race—the most memorable, and perhaps today, the only memorable, sequence in the movie.) It then swept the Academy Awards with twelve nominations, winning eleven of them (the poor screenwriter was the only one not allowed into the post-victory party because he didn't have a statuette to validate as his invitation). *Ben-Hur* is also one of those films that you wonder how it would have turned out had one of the first choices for the title role been signed before Charlton Heston was hired. Supposedly Marlon Brando, Burt Lancaster, and even Rock Hudson were sought as Judah Ben-Hur before Heston. (Talk about four *different* directions for the character of Ben-Hur to take!)

Judah Ben-Hur, prince of Hur, is a rather peaceable man who is trying to make the best of a continuously bad situation: his country occupied (again!) by foreign conquerors. But this time, because he was once friends with one of the Roman tribunes, Ben-Hur gets caught up in the maelstrom of the time and comes up on the short end of the stick. He's arrested for helping Jewish agitators, sold into slavery, does duty as a galley slave during which he saves a prominent Roman commander and is adopted as his son. He then takes revenge upon the man who caused all his misery, Messala, in a turbulent chariot race, ending in Ben-Hur's victory and Messala's death. After that, Ben-Hur has to find his long lost family and peace with himself. This happens when he witnesses the crucifixion of Christ and its aftermath.

The subtitle of *Ben-Hur* is *A Tale Christ* but Jesus of Nazareth plays a very small part in the story, and most of the time Ben-Hur goes about his business as if he's never heard of the former carpenter from Nazareth who is now an itinerant rabbi. The film's scenario does begin with the birth of Christ and ends with his crucifixion and resurrection, but the character that ties all of this together is the aging Balthazar, one of the three original Magi. Balthazar seeks the Christ throughout the picture, rather like King Pellinore in *The Once and Future King*, who keeps chasing after the Questing Beast.

BEN-HUR AND MESSALA

Prince Judah Ben-Hur's boyhood friend, Messala, a Roman, has returned to Judah as a Roman Tribune. Messala left as a boy and has returned as a grown soldier. Ben-Hur has also grown into a man. The joyous reunion Ben-Hur had hoped for, with their friendship resuming where it ended as boys, has not happened. There has been a sour note due to some scrimaging between the Roman occupation forces and the rebel contingency in Judah. Messala has hoped that Ben-Hur will be on his side and that he will see that the future is Rome. Messala hopes that his boyhood friend will have the same view of Judea as he does and that they will rise together. Both men soon realize that they have left more than childhood behind now that they are men.

TWO SHOT—BEN-HUR AND MESSALA

They have approached a stable. There are several horses, among them a fine black Arab stallion. Ben-Hur gestures to the attendant who brings the horse to them.

BEN-HUR
How do you like him?

MESSALA
Magnificent. . . .

Messala examines the horse professionally.

MESSALA
Arabic—

BEN-HUR
(*Nods.*) I think he's got the look of the breed. . . .

MESSALA
Yes! He has the eye.

BEN-HUR
And the heart. I've raced him.

MESSALA
Let me try him. . . .

BEN-HUR
Whenever you like. He's yours.

MESSALA
(*Overcome.*) You . . . you'll *give* me this? Oh, Judah . . . (*He faces Ben-Hur.*) Judah, you are good, and it's going to be like old times. I know it!

Messala embraces Ben-Hur. A warm moment; then:

MESSALA

Tell me . . . Did you . . . did you think about
what I said yesterday?

BEN-HUR

Yes. . . .

MESSALA

And:

BEN-HUR

I have talked to a number of people
already. And I have spoken against
violence, against . . . incidents. Most of the men
I talked to agree with me.

MESSALA

(*Frowning.*) Most . . . but not all?

BEN-HUR

No, not all.

MESSALA

(*Carefully.*) Who does NOT agree?

Ben-Hur pauses uncomfortably; he is evasive.

BEN-HUR

The resentful, the impatient . . .

MESSALA

(*Quickly.*) Who are they? (*Pause.*) Yes, Judah,
who are they?

BEN-HUR

(*Startled at his bluntness.*) Would I retain your
friendship if I became an informer?

MESSALA

To tell me the names of criminals is hardly informing.

BEN-HUR

(*Evenly.*) They are not criminals, Messala. They are patriots. Like you.

MESSALA

Patriots! (*He stops himself; he speaks urgently now, personally.*) Judah, let me explain something to you. Something you may not know. The Emperor is watching us. At this moment he watches the East. This is my great opportunity . . . and yours, too. If I bring order into Judea I can have any post I want . . . and you'll rise with me. I promise. And do you know where it can end? Rome. Yes! Perhaps at the side of Caesar himself. I mean it . . . it can happen, and this is the moment, Judah. I swear: *this is the time*. The Emperor is watching us, judging us. All I must do is serve him. And all you need do is help me—serve Him.

BEN-HUR

(*Slowly.*) You speak as if he were God.

MESSALA

He is god. The only god. He is power. Real power on earth. Not . . . (*Gestures at the sky.*)— not that! (*Then softly.*) Help me, Judah.

BEN-HUR

(*Gently.*) I would do anything for you, Messala, except betray my own people.

MESSALA

(*Explodes.*) In the name of all the gods, what do lives of a few Jews mean to you?

BEN-HUR

(*Sharply.*) If I cannot persuade them, that does
not mean that I will help you murder them.
Besides—you must know this, Messala—I
believe in the past of my people and in their
future.

MESSALA

Future! You are a conquered people. . . .

Their eyes meet in open hostility.

BEN-HUR

(*Intensely.*) You may conquer the land. You may
slaughter the people. But that is not the end. We
will rise again.

MESSALA

(*Rapidly, his voice rising.*) You live on dead
dreams. You live on myths of the past. The glory
of Solomon is gone! Do you think it will return?
Moses is dead! Joshua will not rise again to save
you —nor David. (*A moment, then significantly.*)
There is only one reality in the world today.
Look to the West, Judah. Look to Rome.

*Ben-Hur staets at Messala a moment, understanding at last the division
between them.*

BEN-HUR

(*Slowly.*) I thought it was my friend who had
returned. But I was wrong. It is a conqueror who
has returned. . . . An enemy.

MESSALA

Judah, you're a fool!

Ben-Hur lashes back in anger.

BEN-HUR

I would rather be a fool than a traitor. *Or* a killer.

MESSALA

(*Stung.*) I am a soldier who. . . .

BEN-HUR

(*Fiercely.*) Who kills for Rome. And Rome is evil.

MESSALA

(*Taken back.*) Judah, I warn you. . . .

BEN-HUR

No, I *warn* you. Rome is an affront to God. Rome is strangling my people, my country, the whole earth, but not forever, and I tell you this: the day Rome falls there will be a shout of freedom such as the world has never heard before!

There is a silence. Ben-Hur looks at him in anguish: there is nothing more he can say; he is resolved. Messala sees this.

MESSALA

(*Carefully, coldly.*) Judah, either you help me or you oppose me. You have no other choice. Either you are for me or you are against me.

BEN-HUR

(*With pain.*) If that is the choice, Messala . . . then I am against you.

MESSALA

(*Slowly, with hate, humiliation.*) Remember, I begged you. . . .

Messala turns abruptly and goes. Ben-Hur starts to restrain him, but he is gone.

CLOSE SHOT—BEN-HUR

BEN-HUR
Messala. . . .

But Messala does not look back. The horse on its rein whinnies. Ben-Hur looks at it, recalling this was a gift. He starts to call again, but he does now. Instead, sadly, he strokes the horse's neck. Then he starts back to the house.

BEN-HUR AND IRAS

When Ben-Hur rejected Messala's offer, Messala became a very vindictive enemy. Through circumstances for which Ben-Hur was not really responsible, he and his family were accused by Messela of instigating an incident that was perceived as an attack upon the commander of the Roman garrison. The Ben-Hur family was arrested and separated, their property confiscated by the authorities. Ben-Hur's mother and sister were imprisoned and forgotten, and Ben-Hur himself sold into galley slavery.

During one of the naval battles, Ben-Hur manages to escape the below decks (which are sure death to galley slaves during a sea battle, since the point of the battle seemed to be how many ships one side could ram and sink of the opponents). Being the noble man he is, Ben-Hur takes time out from his escape to save the life of the commander, Arrius. Arrius later takes Ben-Hur to Rome and adopts him as his son.

Somewhere along the way, Ben-Hur has learned how to be a master charioteer and has acquired a reputation for racing chariots. (Amazing what career opportunities are offered to a former galley slave who has a knack for the right networking). When Ben-Hur returns to Judea he is asked by an Arab shiek to race his set of white horses against Messala's black horses (get the symbolism) in the local circus. The Shiek hates Messala, his daughter hates Messala (possibly for some—shall we call it—
"sexual harrassment"?) and of course, Messala is no longer a great favorite of Prince Judah Ben-Hur. So, Ben-Hur jumps at the challenge.

Along the way of his convoluted life, Ben-Hur has also found time to fall in love. Of course the woman is beautiful, but she has also been one of Ben-Hur's own slaves, whom he has freed as a token of his love. But the Shiek's daughter takes one look at Ben-Hur and knows this immediately is a man she wants to know better. After a hard day's training at the practice track, Ben-Hur returns to his tent, hoping to retire for a little rest. However, Ben-Hur has a visitor—and according to Arab customs of the times, this visit ain't exactly kosher.

EXT. TENT—NIGHT

Ben-Hur walks thoughtfully, CAMERA with him, to his own tent. Inside a single lamp is lit, casting a dim golden-glow. Ben-Hur lifts tent flap, enters.

INT. TENT—HIS POINT OF VIEW

Iras is there on a divan. She is unveiled. When she sees him, she gets to her feet, smiling. Ben-Hur is taken aback.

BEN-HUR
I'm sorry. I thought this was the tent. . . .

IRAS
(*Interrupting.*) Your tent. Where you mean to sleep.

Ben-Hur studies her a moment.

BEN-HUR
So I thought.

She smiles. . . .

IRAS
It is your tent. It's quiet and cool. You should sleep well here.

BEN-HUR
(*Moving across to her.*) I've wondered about you while you sat silent . . . what deep thoughts were going on in you mind.

IRAS
My own.

She stoops down and shades the light of a small lamp with her hands, looking across the tent so that her face is in profile to Ben-Hur.

IRAS

You see? The side of the tent is restless: the light
of the flames from the campfire.

Ben-Hur sits on the bed and looks in the direction she indicates; the firelight flickeres through the tent wall.

IRAS

There, how the light dances.

Ben-Hur turns his head and looks at her.

BEN-HUR

Beautiful.

IRAS

Restless, warm. Company in the night.

BEN-HUR

(*Smiling.*) I mean to have sleep for my company.
A dull and necessary sleep.

Iras takes her hands from the lamp, sits beside him.

IRAS

(*After a pause.*) What do you see when you look
at me?

BEN-HUR

A beautiful woman who loves my hatred of
Rome.

IRAS

(*After a beat.*) You mean to race against
Messala.

Ben-Hur gives no answer.

IRAS

I will give you the love to join with your hatred: with these two, no one can beat you. (*She pauses.*) Will you kill Messala?

He is silent for a moment. Her hand touches the slave ring on his finger.

IRAS

Who gave you this ring, Judah?

BEN-HUR

I took it—from a woman who hates my longing to destroy Messala.

IRAS

She isn't worthy of Judah. Is she a slave?

BEN-HUR

She's free.

IRAS

You gave her her freedom. She's worth nothing better. Put the ring on me.

Ben-Hur's hand covers the ring.

IRAS

Put it on me, Judah.

Ben-Hur smiles and rises.

BEN-HUR

It has become a part of my hand.

She rises, turns away from him. After a moment she faces him.

IRAS

(*In a fury of hurt pride.*) So this is what you are!
Slave to a slave who doesn't even know how to
love your anger! She makes you a coward and a
fool! (*She crosses to the tent flap and turns.*)
You, match with Messala! Race with him in the
great circus! You will lose, Judah, just as
you've chosen to lose me. I shall be there to
watch you, as I watch you now. And I know, I
know Messala will defeat you!

She goes. Ben-Hur returns to the divan and throws himself on to it.

BEN-HUR AND PILATE

The first clue you get before the chariot race that Messala is not a fair
sportsman is the presence of large, jagged, sharp blades protruding from the
wheels of his chariot. He employs these to cut the spokes of opposing
chariots as he passes (this man might be accepted by the Olympic
Committee, but he'd be disqualified at the Indianapolis Speedway). Well, of
course, good triumphs, and Ben-Hur wins the race and the accolades. But not
until after an incredibly exciting race. Listen, those cameras set in holes in
the surface of the race track and the horses and chariots thundering over them
will get to anybody—especially the cameramen. But what a price is paid:
Messala is mortally hurt in the race and dies shortly after its conclusion—
thus all bad guys perish.

After the race, Ben-Hur, hero of the hour to everybody, whether they like
him or not, has gone hunting for his mother and sister. They had been thrown
into the darkest hole in the local dungeon and orgotten about—quite literally.
Well, one day, when the jailers are serving up the daily swill, they took a
good look at the two women. Mother and sister Hur had developed leperosy,
and boy did those jailers drop their buckets and scram in horror as fast as
they could. They also shipped the women to a leper colony outside of
civilization with the speed of express mail. (But do not fear. The sacrifice of
Jesus of Nazareth upon the cross also restores mother and sister Hur to full
health, but that's in another part of the picture.)

Ben-Hur persevers in his search for his mother and sister and finally
finds them as lepers. By this time, Ben-Hur is blaming everything on Rome
and on Messala. Ben-Hur has also been summoned to the palace of the
Governor of Judea, Pontius Pilate, who has news for Ben-Hur from his
adopted Roman father, Arrius, who is now one of the Consuls of Rome (a
Consul was the highest elected office in the Roman Empire).

PRAETORIAN HALL—INT. THE GOVERNOR'S PALACE—NIGHT

This is a vaulted chamber with the tribunal of the governor on a dais at one end and under a gilded Roman eagle. Pilate, alone, is reading a scroll. A servant's voice announces:

SERVANT'S VOICE
The prince of Hur.

Pilate comes down from his dias, goes to meet him.

PILATE
I hope I bring you a good conclusion to your day. I have a message for you from the Consul, your father.

BEN-HUR
(*With a reserved sincerity.*) I honor him.

PILATE
As you may honor yourself. You have been made a citizen of Rome.

BEN-HUR
(*His controlled resentment begins to rise.*) I have just come from a valley of stone, my lord Pilate, where my mother and sister live what's left of their lives: by Rome's will—lepers, outcasts without hope.

PILATE
(*With real feeling.*) I have heard this. There was great blame there: very deeply regretted.

BEN-HUR
Their flesh is mine, my lord Pilate: it already carries Rome's mark. The mark is suffering and corrupton.

PILATE

Messala is dead. What he did has had its way
with him.

BEN-HUR

(*With cold, deadly anger.*) The deed was not
Messala's. Rome destroyed Messala, as surely as
Rome has destroyed by family.

PILATE

(*A quiet reasonableness.*) Where there is
greatness—great government, or power—even
great feeling or compassion—error also is great.
We progress and mature by fault. Perfect
freedom, as we know, has no existence. But
Rome has said she is ready to join your life to
hers in a great future. I am sure young Arrius
will choose it.

BEN-HUR

I am Judah Ben-Hur.

Pilate pauses, takes in the significance of Ben-Hur's rejection of Rome.

PILATE

(*Indicating the Tribunal.*) When I go up those
stairs, I become Caesar's representative: I have
already seen and heard, here in Jerusalem, more
than I care for. Even the godmongers are
becoming subversive, like this poor fellow from
Nazareth, setting himself up as a King of the
Jews. (*He comes close to Ben-Hur.*) This
disaffection has come very close to you. You
are a Jew and a Prince. Today you have become
victor and hero to them. They will look to you,
their one true god, as I called you. If you stay
here, you will find yourself part of this tragedy.

BEN-HUR

I am already part of this tragedy. (*He takes the ring off his finger.*) Return this to Arrius. I honor him too well to wear it any longer.

Pilate takes the ring, looks at it and back at Ben-Hur, then goes up the steps to the dais. When he speaks, his voice is impersonal.

PILATE

Even for the sake of Arrius, I can't protect you from personal disaster if you stay here. You're too great a danger to Rome. Leave Judea. You have my warning.

A slight pause, while they face each other. Then Ben-Hur bows abruptly and goes.

ORDER DIRECT